Homemade with Love

Treasured Family Recipes of Marilyn Boyer

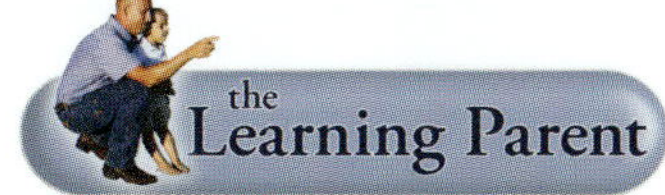

Homemade with Love
Treasured Family Recipes of Marilyn Boyer
by Marilyn Boyer

First printing October, 2013

ISBN: 978-0-9860433-1-4

Published by The Learning Parent
2430 Sunnymeade Road
Rustburg, VA 24588
www.thelearningparent.com

Proudly printed in the United States of America by Jostens

A Word from Marilyn

This cookbook is in response to one of the question I'm most often asked: "What do you feed all those kids?" My answer is: "The same thing you do—only more of it."

When this cookbook was first written in 2000, my husband Rick and I had 14 children, ages 25 years to 21 months. Most of these recipes are quick to fix, as my time is much in demand and I want to spend it with my kids. I often let the younger kids help with food preparation—chopping, peeling, stirring, spreading pizza dough, etc. Some of my fondest memories of my mother are of the times we would spend baking in the kitchen together. A lot of these are treasured family recipes, passed down from generation to generation. I've included personal comments on many of the recipes in this book to help make it more meaningful to you.

As I am revising and planning this second edition, many of my children have grown up and have families of their own. Five are married and we now have 12 grandchildren. I have asked each one of my grown daughters and daughters-in-law to contribute a recipe they make that have now become our new family favorites. We get together as a family every Friday night to share a meal and everyone contributes a dish to share so our favorites have expanded and we want to share that with you. Hope you enjoy the new look and expanded collection of special recipes.

I'm reminded of the words of one of my favorite songs: "We have this moment to hold in our hands, to touch as it slips through our fingers like sand. Yesterday's gone and tomorrow may never come, but we have this moment today."

It is my prayer that you will find recipes in this book that will contribute to building memories as you serve those you love day after day.

Table of Contents

Dedication

I dedicate this cookbook to the family I love most of all in the whole world—a family that has expanded beyond my husband Rick and our 14 children (Rick, Tim, Nate, Josh, Kate, Matt, Emmy, Carrie, Christa, Laura, Grace, Tuck, Kelley, and Kasey) to include our daughters-in-law, (Christina, Kari, and Tina) our sons-in-law, (Kevin and Tim), and our 12 wonderful grandchildren (Cassidy, Luke, Anne, Adam, Melody, Lauren, Patrick, James, Michael, Ella, Lainey, and Autumn). It is my desire to be used of God during my lifetime to help make each one of you successful in God's eyes. Each of you in your own unique way, has made my life so very rich and full and I'm so grateful God has allowed me the opportunity to invest my life in yours.

Cooking is:

tradition, learning, generations, family, fun, memories—

all Homemade with Love!

Cinnamon Roll-Ups

Making cinnamon roll-ups was something my mom always did with my sisters and me after she baked a pie. This is one of my favorite memories of her. We would eat them hot from the oven with a glass of milk, and we always had to save some for Dad when he got home from work. In the summer of 1999, I was back on the Cape with some of my kids, helping to care for my dad, who had cancer and died a few months later. Dad loved rhubarb pie, so one Sunday afternoon, with my daughter Kasey's "help," I baked a rhubarb pie for him and then made cinnamon roll-ups with the leftover pie crust. I was surprised that, even though he had little appetite, he kept sneaking back into the kitchen for one cinnamon roll-up after another until they were all gone!

Roll out leftover pie crust on floured surface to ¼-inch thickness. Spread with a thin layer of margarine and sprinkle generously with cinnamon and sugar. Roll up from the long side. Cut into ½-inch slices. Lay face down in pie pan. Bake about 10 minutes or until lightly browned at 425°.

Cassidy helped "Nana" make cinnamon roll-ups for the first time. It's really great to pass on that tradition that meant so much to me as a child.

Stuffed Tomatoes p. 59

Sweet New England Blueberry Muffins p. 93

Breakfast, Lunch & Snack Ideas

For years, I made a lot of muffins and quick breads for breakfasts. We've always had a garden. Zucchini is always plentiful. I love zucchini bread and muffins. Quick breads can be baked the day before and just sliced and eaten for breakfast in the morning. I would also mix muffin batter the night before and refrigerate it. Then in the morning, all I would have to do is grease the muffin tins, fill, pop in the oven, and go take a bath while they were baking. This makes a very efficient use of time and helps you to still get an early start to your day. Serve with milk or orange julius. I've also made use of a bread machine—filling with ingredients just before bed and setting it to be done when I want it in the morning.

We always seem to run out of lunch ideas, but here are a few of our standbys.

American chop suey
Baked macaroni and cheese
Broccoli rice casserole
Burrito shells stuffed with rice and cheese
Clam chowder
Deli meat sandwiches
Egg salad sandwiches
English muffin pizzas. (Spread sauce on half of split English muffin. Top with grated cheese and pepperoni slices. Broil till cheese is melted.)
French toast
Fried egg sandwiches
Fried rice
Grilled cheese sandwiches
Open-faced Muenster cheese sandwiches
Pita pocket sandwiches with meat and cheese
Potato soup
Raw veggies and dip, crackers and peanut butter (as sides)
Rice and cheese with muffins
Rice casserole
Scrambled eggs
Shrimp, Rice, and Peas—This is one of Kelley's favorites lunches. We buy a bag of precooked shrimp. In a saucepan, melt 2 tsp. margarine and sauté desired amount of shrimp till warmed. Add 2 cups frozen peas and continue stirring till they are warm as well. Serve on rice and sprinkle with cheddar cheese.
Steamed vegetables (broccoli, cauliflower, carrots)
Steamed cabbage and rice with cheese on the side

Steamed summer squash, fresh from the garden, served with cucumber slices dipped in ranch dressing
Stuffed tomatoes
Tuna casserole
Tuna sandwiches

HEALTHY SNACKS

Here's a list of heathy snacks that my daughter compiled. Some we've tried and some we plan to try.

Almonds
Ants on a Log (celery with peanut butter and raisins)
Apple or apple chips
Apple slices dipped in peanut butter or caramel dip (or spread peanut butter on top of apple slice and top with pecans . . . so good!)
Applesauce
Assorted fresh fruit
Baked chips (about 7-10) with salsa
Banana or banana with chocolate drizzle
Banana—frozen (peel it first, stick in the freezer overnight—it's like a yummy popsicle)
Banana Smoothie (½ c. sliced banana, ¼ c. nonfat vanilla yogurt, and a handful of ice blended until smooth)
Blackberries (so good mixed with plain yogurt or Cool Whip)
Bowl of bran flakes with ½ c. skim milk and berries
Cantelope, sliced
Cashews
Chocolate-covered graham crackers
Cheerios, multi-grain
Cheese & crackers
Cheese, string or Cheese wedge—Laughing Cow Light
Cherry tomatoes
Chicken breast, cooked and cubed
Chocolate dipped strawberries
Chocolate milk
Clementines & tangerines
Cottage cheese with mandarin orange slices, pineapple, or sliced peaches
Craisins (I love to eat these with almonds—it's a good combo)
Cucumbers and baby carrots dipped in ranch dip
Dates with almond butter or rolled in coconut
Dried fruits
Egg, hard-boiled
Fruit salsa & cinnamon pita chips
Goldfish crackers or graham crackers
Granola bars
Grapes, fresh or frozen
Green salad (small) with light dressing
Guacamole with veggies
Lime sherbet (½ cup serving) with sliced kiwi
Mango smoothie (frozen mango, mango Greek yogurt, and a small amount of orange juice)
Mixed berry salad (1 cup) (raspberries, strawberries, blueberries,

and/or blackberries) tossed with 1 Tbsp. fresh-squeezed orange juice)
Nuts
Oatmeal
Olives (handful)
Orange slices
Parfait (build your own with yogurt, fruit, and granola)
Peanut butter and bananas on whole wheat bread
Pineapple, fresh
Popcorn
Popsicles—homemade (puree watermelon, strawberries, mango, banana, etc and freeze in popsicle molds)
Pretzels
Protein bar
Pumpkin seeds (2 Tbsp. pumpkin seeds, sprayed with oil (just a spritz!) and baked at for 400° for 15 minutes or until brown)
Quesadilla (whole wheat (or corn) tortillas w/cheese (or not) melted in microwave—adding on tomatoes, beans, corn, olives, avocado or guacamole or whatever sounds good)
Raisins
Rice cakes
Rice Krispie treats
Strawberries—chocolate covered (dip 5 strawberries in 2 squares of dark chocolate)
Sugar snap peas
Sun chips
Sunflower seeds
Sweet potato fries (one light-bulb sized sweet potato sliced, tossed with 1 tsp. olive oil, and baked at 400° for 10 minutes)
Tomatoes, fresh
Tortilla (low-fat) topped with egg salad, shredded carrots and cucumber slices
Tortilla shell with melted cheese and rice inside
Trail mix (make your own! Throw in dried fruit, sunflower seeds, nuts, low-sugar cereals, and even the occasional piece of candy for something sweet)
Triscuits Thin Crisps dipped in cottage cheese or spread with natural peanut butter
Tropical juice smoothie (¼ cup pineapple juice, orange juice, and apple juice, blended with ice)
Veggies, raw
Watermelon
Whole wheat bread
Yogurt, low-fat
Yoplait Whips Yogurt—Frozen (these seriously taste like ice cream when they are frozen!)

Bread & Butter Pickles p. 13

Homemade Strawberry Jam p. 14

Chocolate Chip Cheeseball p. 13

Appetizers, Jams & Pickles

Appetizers, Jams & Pickles

Mom's Clam Dip

This is my very favorite dip!

1 (8 oz.) pkg. cream cheese
1 can minced clams
2 dashes of Worcestershire sauce
2 shakes of onion salt
2 shakes of garlic salt
liquid from minced clams

Mash cream cheese, gradually adding portion of liquid from clams until right consistency. Add all other ingredients; mix well. Drain remaining liquid off clams; add clams and mix thoroughly. Chill until serving time. Serve with potato chips. Store leftovers in refrigerator.

Taco Dip

This is a recipe I got from my sister. It's great.

1 can Fritos bean dip
1 avocado, mashed with fresh garlic
1 pt. sour cream mixed with
  2 pkg. taco seasoning
shredded Cheddar cheese
chopped tomatoes
chopped black olives

Layer, bottom to top in a 9 x 13-inch pan. Serve with chips.

Ihlene's Sour Cream Dip

This is yummy! Great with veggies fresh from the garden.

1 c. mayonnaise
1 c. sour cream
½ Tbsp. Season-All salt (optional)
1 Tbsp. dill weed
3 Tbsp. parsley flakes
3 Tbsp. minced onion

Combine sour cream and mayonnaise; add remaining ingredients. Mix well. Serve with raw vegetables. Store in refrigerator. YIELD: 2 cups.

Pizza Dip

1 (8 oz.) pkg. cream cheese
1 tsp. dried Italian seasoning
1 c. shredded Mozzarella
¾ c. shredded Parmesan cheese
1 (8 oz.) jar pizza sauce
2 tbsp. chopped green bell peppers
2 tbsp. green onion slices

Combine cream cheese and Italian seasoning. Spread onto bottom of pan. Combine both cheeses. Sprinkle ½ over cream cheese mixture. Spread pizza sauce over the top. Top with remaining cheese. Add green pepper and onion slices. Bake 15 minutes or so. Serve warm with Wheat Thins or your favorite crackers.

Chocolate Chip Cheeseball

1 (8 oz.) package cream cheese
½ c. butter
1 tsp. vanilla
¾ c. confectioners' sugar
1 pkg. mini chocolate chips, divided

Beat first three ingredients together. Add sugar and ¾ of the chocolate chips. Form mixture into a ball. Chill. Once chilled, roll in remaining chocolate chips. Serve with Wheat Thins or graham cracker sticks.

Bread and Butter Pickles

4 lb. cucumbers, sliced
3 onions, sliced
½ c. coarse salt
5 c. sugar
5 c. cider vinegar
1 ½ tsp. turmeric
1 ½ tsp. celery seed

Cover cucumbers, onions, and salt with cold water and ice cubes. Let sit about 3 hours. Do not use metal container. Mix sugar, vinegar, turmeric, and celery seed and simmer 30 minutes. Pour cold water off cucumbers and pack in jars; cover with hot liquid. Process 10 minutes in hot water bath.

Homemade Strawberry Jam

5 ⅓ c. crushed strawberries
1⅓ c. water
6 Tbsp. low/no sugar pectin
2 cups sugar
1 Tbsp. butter
8 cleaned and sterilized half pint jars

Wash strawberries and crush in a large bowl with a potato masher. Combine crushed berries along with the water in a large, heavy bottom pan. On medium high heat, gradually add pectin while stirring with a wooden spoon. Add the sugar. Add the butter (butter reduces foaming).
Bring to a hard boil and boil 1 minute stirring constantly. Remove from heat.
Ladle the hot jam into prepared jars, leaving ¼-inch headspace.

Wipe rims with clean damp cloth. Place hot lids on jar and apply rings till tight. Process in hot water bath leaving a little space between each jar. Cover with 1 to 2 inches of water. Cover pot and turn on medium high heat. When the water comes to a boil, time them for 10 minutes at a steady slow boil. Turn off pan and let sit 5 minutes. Then take jars out. Place on a dish towel on countertop and let sit for 24 hours before disturbing. Yields 8 (8 oz.) half pint jars. Enjoy!

Hearty Chicken Cheese Chowder p. 17

Layered Salad p. 21

Cherry Jello Salad p. 21

Ruby Red Raspberry Sauce p. 28

Soups, Salads & Sauces

Soups, Salads & Sauces

Garden Chowder

This thick, creamy chowder makes a good lunch.

½ c. chopped green pepper
½ c. chopped onion
¼ c. butter or margarine
¼ c. each: diced potato, celery, cauliflower, carrot, and broccoli
3 c. water
3 c. chicken bouillon cubes
1 tsp. salt
¼ tsp. pepper
½ c. all-purpose flour
2 c. milk
1 Tbsp. minced fresh parsley
3 c. (12 oz.) shredded Cheddar cheese

In a Dutch oven or soup kettle, sauté green pepper and onion in butter until tender. Add vegetables, water, bouillon, salt, and pepper; bring to a boil. Reduce heat; cover and simmer for 20 minutes or until the vegetables are tender. Combine flour and milk until smooth; stir into pan. Bring to a boil; cook and stir for 2 minutes. Add the parsley. Just before serving, stir in the cheese until melted. YIELD: 6 to 8 servings (2 quarts).

New England Clam Chowder

I grew up on Cape Cod. We would walk across the street to the harbor and dig our own clams. It was my job to scrub them clean in the little corner sink. This is my Mom's recipe.

3 to 4 c. shucked or steamed chowder clams (with their juice or broth)
1 ½-inch cube salt pork, diced small
1 onion, chopped fine
2 Tbsp. flour
3 medium potatoes, peeled and diced
3 c. milk
3 Tbsp. butter
salt
freshly ground pepper

Measure the clam juice or broth from the shucked or steamed clams and add water, if necessary, to make 2½ cups. Cut the clams in small pieces and set aside. Cook the salt pork slowly in a small skillet until the fat has melted and the scraps are brown. Strain; set aside the scraps and put 2 tablespoons of the fat in a large pot. Heat the fat. Add the onion and cook slowly until golden. Sprinkle the flour over the onion and cook, stirring, for 3 minutes. Add the potatoes and clam juice or broth. Cover and simmer 10 minutes. Add the clams and simmer 10 minutes more or until the clams are cooked and the potatoes are tender. Add the milk, butter, and salt and pepper to taste and heat until the butter has melted. Serve with a few crisp pork bits in each bowl.

Hearty Chicken Cheese Chowder

This is Christa's specialty. She often makes it with homemade rolls.

2 chicken bouillon cubes
  or 2 cups chicken broth
2 c. diced potatoes
½ c. sliced carrots
½ c. sliced celery
¼ c. chopped onion
1 ½ tsp. salt
¼ tsp. pepper
2 c. (8 oz.) shredded Cheddar cheese
¼ c. butter or margarine
2 c. milk
1 c. diced, cooked chicken
½ c. flour

Dissolve bouillon cubes in 2 cups boiling water; add vegetables and seasonings. Cover; simmer 10 minutes. Do not drain. Melt butter in saucepan; add flour and blend. Add milk gradually and cook over low heat, stirring constantly until thickened. Add cheese; stir until melted. Add chicken and undrained vegetables. Heat; do not boil. Serve hot.

Grannie's Potato Soup

My kids always beg Rick's mom to make this whenever she comes to visit. My son Josh declared, "Grannie makes the best potato soup in the world!"

8 to 10 medium potatoes, peeled and cut in 1-inch pieces
salt to taste
1 ½ large onions, cut in 1-inch pieces
approximately 1 qt. milk
¼ stick butter
4 to 5 slices bacon

Cover the first 3 ingredients with 4 to 5-inches of water. Boil until tender. Add the milk and butter. Cook the bacon until crisp; chop up and add to soup. Simmer for 5 to 10 minutes.
Variation: Add 2 cups shredded Cheddar cheese with the bacon.

Blueberry Jello Salad

2 small (3 oz.) pkg. raspberry gelatin
1 can crushed pineapple, drained
1 cup boiling water
1 can blueberry pie filling

Dissolve gelatin in boiling water. Add pie filling and drained pineapple. Refrigerate until congealed. Spread topping on salad when congealed; refrigerate until serving time.

Topping:
8 oz. cream cheese
1 c. sour cream
½ c. sugar
1 c. chopped nuts

Beat cream cheese with sour cream and sugar until smooth; spread on salad. Sprinkle with nuts. YIELD: 12 servings.

Molded Strawberry Salad

1 (6 oz.) pkg strawberry gelatin
1 ½ c. boiling water
1 (10 oz.) pkg frozen sweetened strawberries, thawed
1 (8¼ oz.) can crushed pineapple (undrained)
1 c. (8 oz.) sour cream
leaf lettuce and fresh strawberries (optional)

In a bowl, dissolve gelatin in water. Add strawberries and pineapple. Strain, reserving liquid and fruit. Set aside 1 cup of the liquid at room temperature. Pour fruit and remaining liquid into a 5-cup mold or 9-inch square pan that has been coated with nonstick cooking spray. Cover and refrigerate until set, about 1 hour. Whisk sour cream and reserved liquid; pour over top. Cover and refrigerate until set. Unmold onto a serving platter or cut into squares and place on individual plates. Garnish with lettuce and strawberries, if desired. YIELD: 8 servings.

Cranberry Raspberry Jello Salad

My daughter-in-law, Tina, made this one night for family night and boy, is it ever good! I immediately asked her for the recipe.

1 can (20 oz.) crushed pineapple
2 small (3 oz.) or 1 (6 oz.) pkg. raspberry Jello
1 (16 oz.) can whole berry cranberry sauce
1 apple, chopped
⅔ c. chopped walnuts or pecans
1 (16 oz.) can mandarin oranges

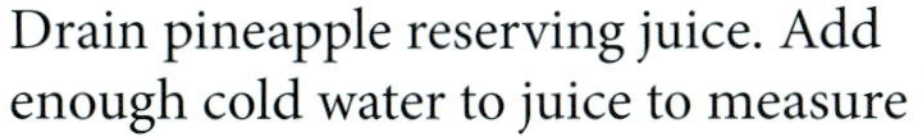

Drain pineapple reserving juice. Add enough cold water to juice to measure 3 cups. Pour into saucepan. Bring to boil and remove from heat. Add dry Jello mixes. Stir 2 minutes. Stir in cranberry sauce. Pour into large bowl. Refrigerate 1½ hours or until slightly thickened. Stir in pineapple, apple, oranges, nuts. Refrigerate until firm.

Sour Cream Salad

1 (6-serving size) pkg. lime gelatin
½ c. pecans, chopped
1 c. crushed pineapple, drained
1 pt. sour cream
2 c. boiling water

Dissolve gelatin in boiling water; allow to cool. Stir in sour cream thoroughly (cottage cheese may be substituted if desired, but sour cream tastes best). Add crushed pineapple and nuts. Chill. YIELD: 18 servings.

Orange Pineapple Salad

This recipe has been a favorite of my son Matt for years. You can change the flavor of jello as desired.

2 small cans crushed pineapple, drained
1 can mandarin oranges, drained
1 large carton cottage cheese
2 small pkg. orange gelatin (dry)
1 large carton Cool Whip

Mix well. Refrigerate at least 15 to 30 minutes before serving. YIELD: 8 to 10 servings.

Ambrosia Salad

This is our holiday fruit salad. It's a must for Thanksgiving and Christmas dinners.

1 can crushed pineapple
1 can mandarin oranges
1 ½ c. sour cream
2 cans fruit cocktail
1 c. coconut
1 (10 oz.) pkg minature marshmallows

Drain fruit. Combine all ingredients and refrigerate until serving time.

Cherry Jello Salad

This is so yummy! We serve this dish for company a lot, everyday dinners and for cookouts in the summer. *(See photo on page 15.)*

2 small pkg. cherry gelatin
2 c. boiling water
1 can crushed pineapple
1 can cherry pie filling

Dissolve gelatin in boiling water. Drain pineapple. Add cherry pie filling and pineapple to gelatin. Stir well; pour into 9 x 13-inch pan and refrigerate until serving time (at least 3 to 4 hours). YIELD: 12 to 14 servings.

Optional Topping:

8 oz. softened cream cheese
1 c. sour cream
½ c. sugar

Beat together until smooth; spread over top of congealed salad.

Layered Salad

6 large eggs
12 strips lean bacon
2 tomatoes, diced (about 2 lb.)
1 (10 oz.) box frozen peas, thawed and drained
8 oz. extra-sharp Cheddar, shredded or diced (2 cups)
⅓ c. pitted black olives
2 (5 oz.) bags mixed greens
½ c. ranch dressing

Place eggs in a medium saucepan with cold water to cover. Bring to a simmer over medium heat. Remove from heat, cover pan and let stand for 10 minutes. Drain eggs and cool in ice water. Peel and set aside.

Cook bacon in batches in a large, heavy skillet over medium heat until crisp, about 10 minutes. Drain on paper towels. Tear bacon into pieces.

Arrange tomatoes, peas, Cheddar, olives, greens and bacon in layers in a large (5-quart), clear bowl with straight sides.

Just before serving, quarter eggs and place on top. Serve with dressing on side or toss.

Patriotic Jello Salad

My friend Bev said she thinks of me whenever she makes this scrumptious Jello salad. Got to be one of my favorites and it looks so patriotic too!

1 package (3 oz.) berry blue Jello
2 cups boiling water, (divided in half)
2 ½ cups cold water, (divided into 1 cup, 1 cup, and ½ cup)
1 cup fresh blueberries
1 envelope unflavored gelatin
1 cup heavy whipping cream
6 tablespoons sugar
2 cups (16 oz.) sour cream
1 teaspoon vanilla extract
1 package (3 oz.) strawberry or raspberry Jello
1 cup fresh strawberries , sliced, or raspberries if you wish
1 (8 oz.) container of Cool Whip

In a bowl, dissolve berry blue gelatin in 1 cup boiling water and then stir in 1 cup cold water. Pour into a large glass trifle bowl. Sprinkle with blueberries and refrigerate until firm, about 1 to 2 hours.

In a saucepan, sprinkle unflavored gelatin over ½ cup cold water and let stand about 1 minute. Add the cream and sugar and stir over low heat until gelatin and sugar are completely dissolved.

When cool whisk in the sour cream and vanilla.

Carefully spoon over the blue layer and refrigerate until firm, about 1 to 2 hours.

In a bowl, dissolve strawberry or raspberry Jello with remaining hot water and stir in remaining cold water. Carefully spread/spoon over cream layer and sprinkle with strawberries or raspberries. Chill until set, about 1 to 2 hours.

Garnish with Cool Whip and berries on top and refrigerate until ready to serve. Enjoy!

Tropical Salad

We make this recipe in the winter time when fresh fruit is hard to get.

1 (20 oz.) can chunk pineapple
1 can mandarin oranges
1 large banana
1 large or 2 small pkg. vanilla instant pudding*

*Kroger or Royal brands are best.

Drain pineapple and oranges, reserve juice. Combine juice and dry instant pudding. Add pineapple and oranges. Chill well. Add slices banana just before serving. YIELD: 6 to 8 servings.

BLT Macaroni Salad

This is so good. One of my friends brings this to our Independence Day Party each year and I look forward to it!

2 cups uncooked elbow macaroni
5 green onions, finely chopped
1 large tomato diced
1¼ c. diced celery
1¼ c. mayonnaise
5 tsp. white vinegar
¼ tsp. salt
¼ tsp pepper
1 lb. bacon, crumbled

Cook macaroni. In bowl combine macaroni, onions, tomatoes, and celery. In small bowl combine mayo, vinegar, salt and pepper. Pour over macaroni mixture and toss to coat. Cover and chill for 2 hours. Just before serving add bacon.

Mom's Italian Spaghetti Sauce

Mom and I both loved spaghetti. I remember her making and freezing this sauce. When we'd eat it on spaghetti throughout the year, Mom and I would pile our plates high!

Approximately 24 cups tomatoes
2 or 3 onions (or more, if desired), chopped
2 pieces garlic (from clove of garlic)
green peppers to taste
spearmint to taste—I use one leaf
1 tsp. salt
2 Tbsp. sugar
2 tsp. Worcestershire sauce
1 Tbsp. oregano
about 2 Tbsp. olive oil

Wash tomatoes and cut in pieces. Put in large quart pan and add onions. Add garlic, green peppers, spearmint, salt, sugar, Worcestershire sauce, oregano, and olive oil. Bring to a boil. Then turn heat down to low and simmer, being careful not to scorch on bottom, for 2 hours or until tender and boiled down about a fourth of the way on the pan. Strain through strainer and return to a clean pan and boil once again until thickened a little more. Pour into plastic containers and cool. Then freeze.

When preparing spaghetti, heat sauce and add margarine and Parmesan cheese to taste. A can of tomato paste may be added if sauce needs thickening.

Coleslaw

Our daughter-in-law Tina makes this coleslaw for many of our cookouts. The following is her note:
"For the coleslaw I honestly don't have a recipe. I just eyeball it and taste test. Here are approximate measurements. Maybe a trial run would be in order to see if it turns out!"

1 head cabbage, shredded
2 carrots, shredded
4 Tbsp. vinegar
3 Tbsp. sugar
¾ c. mayonnaise
2 tsp. horseradish

Mix all ingredients, and refrigerate to blend flavors.

Garden Fresh Pizza Sauce

My daughter Grace makes this every summer with fresh tomatoes from our garden and we look forward to using it all year long.

28 oz. skinned and crushed tomatoes (We usually puree in blender.)
Skin tomatoes easily by first plunging in boiling water until skins just begin to crack and peel. Then plunge into a clean sink full of ice water. Skins will slide off easily with a knife.
2 cans (6 oz. each) tomato paste
½ c. water
2 Tbsp. sugar
1 ½ tsp. dried basil
1 ½ tsp. dried oregano
1 tsp. garlic powder
¼ tsp. salt
¼ tsp. ground pepper
1 ½ tsp. parsley

In large pan combine tomatoes, tomato paste, water, sugar, basil, oregano, garlic powder, and salt. Bring to a boil. Reduce heat; simmer uncovered for approximately 3 hours until sauce reaches desired thickness, stirring occasionally. Stir in pepper; cook 5 minutes longer. You can use immediately on pizza or can in a boiling water bath for 10 minutes for pints and quarts.

Sweet and Sour Sauce

¾ c. sugar
½ c. ketchup
1 tsp. salt
⅔ c. water
½ c. vinegar

Combine in saucepan. Warm and add thickening:

Thickening:

3½ Tbsp. cornstarch
⅓ c. water

Cook until thick and clear.

Pecan Caramel Sauce

My daughter-in-law Kari makes this delicious ice cream topping. Umm. Good!

½ c. butter
1 ½ c. firmly packed brown sugar
2 Tbsp. light corn syrup
½ c. whipping cream
¼ c. chopped pecans

In medium saucepan, melt butter. Stir in brown sugar and corn syrup. Bring to a boil; cook until sugar is dissolved, stirring constantly. Stir in whipping cream; return to a boil. Remove from heat; stir in pecans. Serve warm over ice cream.

Gram's Hot Fudge Sauce

Mom made this for a special treat. It's real thick.

3 sq. unsweetened baking chocolate
1 can sweetened condensed milk
1 tsp. vanilla

Combine chocolate squares and condensed milk in double boiler over medium-low heat. Cook and stir until chocolate is melted and sauce is smooth and thick. Add vanilla; stir well. Serve hot over ice cream or other desserts.

Fudge Sauce

6 Tbsp. butter
1 c. sugar
1 c. cocoa
pinch of salt
1 c. whipping cream
1 tsp. vanilla extract

In medium saucepan, melt 6 Tbsp. butter. Stir in 1 c. sugar, 1 c. cocoa, and a pinch of salt. Gradually stir in 1 c. whipping cream. Heat, stirring constantly, until smooth and hot but not boiling. Remove from heat; stir in 1 tsp. vanilla extract. YIELD: 2 cups.

Ruby Red Raspberry Sauce

This recipe is one of our daughter-in-law Kari's specialties. Family members often request it for birthday parties. So good!

2 packages of frozen raspberries (about 12 to16 oz. each) or use fresh raspberries—at least 4 cups

juice from half of a whole lemon

12 Tbsp. sugar

4 Tbsp. seedless raspberry jelly

In a food processor, add the raspberries and then process until smooth. Add the raspberries to a sauté pan and then add the other ingredients. Heat on medium heat, and stir frequently (almost constantly) until it thickens up. Then, get a mesh strainer and place it over a bowl. Pour the raspberry sauce through the strainer.

Now, the sauce is not going to just flow right through because the seeds are going to get in the way. So you will need to keep stirring the sauce, which will help it through the strainer. When you cannot get any more sauce to come through, discard the remaining seeds. You should now have approximately three cups of a beautiful red raspberry sauce. Allow it to cool a bit before serving. Or, refrigerate, sealed tightly, until you are ready to serve. I think it tastes awesome still a little warm, or icy cold—it's your preference!

Homemade Pizza p. 57
Baked Almond Chicken p. 46
Little Cheddar Meat Loaves p. 32

Meats & Main Dishes

Meats & Main Dishes

Beef au Jus

Our daughter-in-law Tina made this for the family on one of our family beach trips. Delicious and loved by all.

1 boneless beef or venison roast (approximately 4 lbs.)
2 Tbsp. vegetable oil
2 large sweet onions, cut into ¼-inch slices
6 Tbsp. butter, softened, divided
5 c. water
½ c. soy sauce
1 envelope onion soup mix
1 garlic clove, minced
1 loaf French bread, or sandwich rolls
1 c. shredded mozzarella

In Dutch oven over medium-high heat, brown roast on all sides in oil; drain. In large skillet, saute onion in 2 Tbsp. of butter until tender. Add the water, soy sauce, soup mix, and garlic. Pour over roast. Cover and bake at 325° for 2½ hours or until meat is tender. Let sit 10 minutes before slicing. Return meat to pan juices. Slice bread in half lengthwise; cut into 3-inch sections. Spread remaining butter over bread. Place on a baking sheet. Broil 4-6 inches from the heat for 2-3 minutes or until golden brown. Top with beef and onions; sprinkle with cheese. Broil 4-6 inches from the heat for 1-2 minutes or until cheese is melted. Serve with pan juices.

Crock-Pot Roast and Gravy

This is one of my easiest meals to prepare. Put in the crock-pot around noon, run your errands, and a wonderful meal is done by 5 or 6 PM. If you have a large enough crock-pot, you can add potatoes and carrots.

1 chuck roast
1 pkg onion soup mix
1 can cream of mushroom soup
2 c. water

Place roast in crock-pot. Combine mushroom soup, onion soup mix, and water; whisk. Pour over roast. (This makes a gravy as it cooks.) Cook on high 5 to 6 hours.

Pepperjack Meatloaf

Our daughter-in-law Kari brought this tasty meatloaf for one of our family night dinners and ever since it's been on the list of favorites!

1 egg
1 c. seasoned bread crumbs
¼ c. chopped onion
½ to 1 tsp. salt
½ tsp. pepper
1 ½ pounds lean ground beef (90% lean)
1 c. (4 oz.) pepper Jack cheese, divided

In a large bowl, combine the egg, bread crumbs, onion, salt and pepper. Crumble beef over mixture and mix well. Press half of the beef mixture onto the bottom and halfway up the sides of a greased 8 x 4-inch loaf pan. Sprinkle ¾ cup cheese over meat to within ½ inch of sides. Pat remaining beef mixture over cheese. Bake, uncovered, at 350° for 50-55 minutes or until meat is no longer pink and a meat thermometer reads 160°. Sprinkle with remaining cheese. Bake 5 minutes longer or until cheese is melted. Let stand for 10 minutes before slicing. YIELD: 6 servings.

Little Cheddar Meat Loaves

These are very good and go a long way!

1 egg
¾ c. milk
1 c. (4 oz.) shredded Cheddar cheese
½ c. quick-cooking oats
½ c. chopped onion
1 ½ tsp. prepared mustard (optional)
1 tsp. salt
1 lb. lean ground beef
⅔ c. ketchup
½ c. brown sugar

In a bowl, beat the egg and milk. Stir in cheese, oats, onion, and salt. Add beef and mix well. Shape into 8 loaves; place in a greased 9 x 13-inch baking dish. Combine ketchup, brown sugar, and mustard, if desired; spoon over loaves. Bake, uncovered, at 350° for 45 minutes or until the meat is no longer pink and meat thermometer reads 160°. YIELD: 8 servings.

Make-Ahead Meatballs

This is one of our favorite meatball recipes. It makes a lot. They can be frozen and used in several different recipes, or just eaten as a main dish and served with potatoes and vegetables.

4 eggs
2 c. dry bread crumbs or quick oats
½ c. chopped onion
1 Tbsp. salt
2 tsp. Worcestershire sauce
½ tsp. white pepper
4 lb. lean ground beef

In a large bowl, beat eggs. Add the next 5 ingredients. Add beef; mix well. Shape into balls, about 12 dozen. Place in single layers in ungreased 15 x 10 x 1-inch baking pans. Bake at 400° for 10 to 15 minutes or until no longer pink, turning often; drain. Cool. Place about 30 meatballs each into freezer containers. May be frozen for up to 3 months. YIELD: 5 batches (about 30 meatballs per batch).

Cheese Meatballs

Another meatball favorite. We often have these with scalloped potatoes and veggies.

1 lb. ground beef
2 Tbsp. onion, chopped fine
1 c. grated cheese
1 Tbsp. parsley, chopped fine or
  1 ½ tsp. dried parsley flakes
1 egg, beaten
½ c. breadcrumbs or
  wheat germ
½ tsp. salt

Preheat over to 350°. Mix all ingredients with a fork in a bowl. Shape meat into 30 to 40 meatballs, about 1-inch in diameter. Arrange on baking sheet, 1-inch apart. Bake for 25 minutes. YIELD: 30 to 40 meatballs.

Meatball Sandwiches

1 batch 30 meatballs (frozen or thawed)
1 c. ketchup
¾ c. packed brown sugar
¼ to ½ c. chopped onion
¼ tsp. garlic powder
⅛ tsp liquid smoke (optional)
6 sandwich rolls, split

Place meatballs in an ungreased 1-quart baking dish. Combine the next 5 ingredients; pour over meatballs. Cover and bake at 350° for 1 hour. Serve on rolls. Meatballs may also be served on toothpicks as appetizers. YIELD: 6 servings.

Mom's Rice Meatballs

My mom served this as we were growing up. I've also heard them called "Porcupine Meatballs."

1 lb. ground beef
1 c. cooked Minute rice
2 tsp. salt
1 egg
⅛ tsp. pepper
2 ½ c. tomato juice, divided

Combine meat, rice, salt, egg, pepper, and ½ cup tomato juice. Mix and form into 18 round balls. Place in large frying pan; cover with 2 cups tomato juice. Cook over low heat, turning once, until done, 20 to 30 minutes. YIELD: 18 meatballs.

Chili

This is my husband's favorite and it's quite original! I never had chili growing up. I'd only heard stories of chili con carne my dad had been served while he was in the Navy, and being from the North, I thought he was saying "chili corn carne," hence the addition of corn. My husband loved it and the kids did, too, and that's been a favorite main dish for 40 years now.

2 lb. ground beef
1 tsp. minced onion
garlic powder to taste
5 cans pinto beans
1 (16 oz.) can tomato sauce
1 can corn, drained, or the equivalent in frozen corn
1 ½ Tbsp. chili powder

Put ground beef in large pan or Dutch oven. Add minced onion and garlic powder to taste. Brown, then drain off the grease. Add pinto beans, tomato sauce, and corn. Add chili powder. Bring to a boil, then simmer for about 30 minutes. Serve in bowls topped with shredded Cheddar cheese and saltine crackers, crushed or broken in small pieces, and ketchup, if desired.

We often serve cornbread on the side.

Green Chili Casserole

I got this easy recipe from my mother-in-law.

1 lb. hamburger
1 can diced green chilies
1 small pkg. Doritos
diced onion
1 can cream of mushroom soup
shredded Longhorn or Cheddar cheese

Brown hamburger, onion, and green chilies (drain first). Then stir in cream of mushroom soup. Line pan with half the Doritos; add soup mixture. Add the rest of the Doritos; sprinkle with cheese. Bake at 350° until cheese is melted and bubbling.

Barbecue Meatballs

These are delicious. We have them often.

1 lb. ground beef
¾ c. quick oatmeal
½ c. milk
2 Tbsp. onion flakes
salt and pepper to taste

Mix all ingredients and form into balls the size of a quarter.

Sauce:

1 c. ketchup
2 Tbsp. brown sugar
½ c. water
2 Tbsp. vinegar
2 Tbsp. onion flakes
2 Tbsp. Worcestershire sauce

Mix sauce ingredients well. Place browned meatballs in baking dish. Pour sauce over and bake at 350° for approximately 1 hour.

Hamburger Tomato Pie

One of my mom's favorites.

1 ½ lb. ground beef
1 large can tomatoes
2 cans green beans
2 cans corn, drained
mashed potatoes
grated cheese

Brown and drain the ground beef. Place in 9 x 13-inch pan. Add tomatoes, green beans, and corn. Top with mashed potatoes and grated cheese. Bake at 350° for 10 to 15 minutes.

Taco Ring

We often have this on a Saturday evening; little preparation time is required.

1 pkg. crescent rolls
½ lb. ground beef
½ to 1 pkg. taco seasoning
1 c. shredded cheese
2 Tbsp. water

Cook and drain beef; add ½ to 1 package of taco seasoning according to your taste, cheese, and water. Lay crescent rolls on baking sheet; fill with meat mixture and fold over. Seal edges. Bake at 375° for 20 to 25 minutes. Serve with lettuce, diced tomatoes, and sour cream, if desired.

Mexican Casserole

This is easy to make and tastes wonderful.

1 lb. ground beef
1 pkg. taco seasoning
chopped onion
1 can refried beans
green onions, chopped
tomatoes, diced
ripe olives, sliced
sour cream
grated Cheddar cheese

Brown beef with onions. Drain; add taco seasoning. Simmer. Spray 9 x 13-inch pan with nonstick cooking spray. Spread refried beans in the bottom of pan as the first layer. Add meat mixture as second layer; then green onions, tomatoes, olives, sour cream, and cheese. Bake at 350° until heated through. Serve with lettuce and taco sauce or salsa, if desired, as a main dish, or as a dip for taco or corn chips.

Hamburger Chow Mein Casserole

1 ½ lb. hamburger
1 medium onion
1 c. diced celery
2 cans cream of mushroom soup
1 can chicken rice soup
1 (No. 303) can mixed vegetables (do not drain)
2 c. chow mein noodles
2 tsp. soy sauce
1 (4 oz.) can mushroom pieces

Brown hamburger with onion. Add remaining ingredients. Turn into a 3-quart casserole and bake at 350° for 1 hour.

Salisbury Steak

1 lb. ground beef
¼ c. green pepper, chopped
¼ c. chopped onion
1 egg
½ tsp. chili powder
1 slice bread
1 pkg. brown gravy mix fixed according to directions on package

Wet bread in water; squeeze water out. Mix all ingredients and form into patties 1-inch thick. Fry slowly until done in the middle. Simmer in brown gravy.

Classic Lasagna

We have pasta every Wednesday night and this is one of our favorites.

1 ½ lb. ground beef
¾ c. chopped onion
1 (16 oz.) can tomatoes
2 (6 oz.) cans tomato paste
2 c. water
1 Tbsp. chopped parsley
2 tsp. salt
1 tsp. sugar
1 tsp. garlic powder
½ tsp. pepper
½ tsp. oregano
½ tsp. basil
8 oz. lasagna noodles
2 (8 oz.) pkg. Mozzarella cheese slices

Cheese layer:

1 c. Parmesan cheese
1 c. Ricotta or cottage cheese
2 eggs

Brown ground beef and onion, drain. Add tomatoes, tomato paste, water, oregano, pepper, and basil. Simmer, uncovered, stirring occasionally for 30 minutes.

Mix Ricotta cheese, Parmesan cheese, and eggs. Cook lasagna noodles. In a 9 x 13-inch pan, place a layer of noodles. Spread on half the cheese mixture, then a layer of Mozzarella and half the meat sauce. Repeat layers, ending with meat sauce, and garnish with remaining Mozzarella cheese slices. Bake at 350° for 35 minutes. Let stand 15 minutes before serving. YIELD: 8 to 12 servings.

Mock Lasagna

We first had this when a Mennonite friend brought us a meal after we had a baby. It's fast, easy, and good!

1 ½ lb. ground beef or sausage
1 lb. spaghetti
1 ½ c. cottage cheese
1 ½ c. grated Mozzarella cheese
1 jar spaghetti sauce

Brown the ground beef or sausage. Drain. Cook the spaghetti; drain. Add browned meat, cottage cheese, Mozzarella cheese and spaghetti sauce.

American Chop Suey

A recipe my mom made frequently. It mixes up for a quick supper or lunch.

1 lb. ground beef
1 lb. elbow macaroni
2 cans tomato soup
grated cheese (if desired)

Brown ground beef; drain. Cook macaroni until tender; drain. Add ground beef, soup, and cheese, if desired.

Cornbread Tamale Pie

Easy and tasty. A good Saturday night supper.

1 lb. ground beef
1 chopped onion
1 can tomato soup
1 c. water
¼ tsp. pepper
1 tsp. salt
1 Tbsp. chili powder
1 can drained corn
½ c. green pepper

Sauté ground beef and onion. Add tomato soup, water, pepper, salt, chili powder, corn, and ground pepper. Simmer 15 minutes.

Cornbread Topping:

¾ c. cornmeal
1 Tbsp. flour
1 Tbsp. sugar
½ tsp. salt
½ tsp. baking powder
1 beaten egg
⅓ c. milk
1 Tbsp. cooking oil

Mix cornmeal, flour, sugar, salt, and baking powder. Moisten with egg and milk. Mix lightly and fold in oil. Place meat mixture in greased 2-quart casserole. Cover with cornbread topping. Topping will disappear into meat mixture, but will rise during baking. Bake 20 to 25 minutes at 425°.

Meat Loaf and Potatoes

1 lb. hamburger
2 eggs
2 pieces cubed bread
onions
4 to 5 potatoes, peeled and chopped
¼ c. ketchup

Mix together hamburger, eggs, cubed bread and onions. Press into a standard bread pan (approximately 10 ½ x 5 ¼ x 2 ¾ inches). Chop potatoes; scatter them around the meatloaf. Add water around the sides, on top of the potatoes, but not on top of the meat. Spread the ketchup on top of meat loaf. Cover with aluminum foil. Bake at 350° for about an hour.

Sloppy Joes

Large yield and very tasty! I got this recipe from my son's mother-in-law.

4 lb. ground beef
½ of a 24 oz. bottle ketchup
2 Tbsp. vinegar
3 Tbsp. brown sugar
touch of barbecue sauce (optional)
15-20 hamburger buns

Brown ground beef with onions. Add ketchup, vinegar, brown sugar, and barbecue sauce; simmer 30 minutes or until hot. Serve on buns. YIELD: 15 to 20 servings.

Creamed Hamburger on Toast

This was served to Rick when he was in the Air Force. He really liked it, so we made up our own recipe from his description. It makes a super quick Saturday night supper.

2 lb. ground beef
salt, pepper, garlic powder, & onion powder
1 stick margarine
8 Tbsp. flour
3 c. milk
2 cans drained peas (if desired)

Brown ground beef seasoned with salt, pepper, garlic powder, and onion powder in skillet. Drain. Meanwhile, make a white sauce by melting margarine in saucepan. When melted stir in flour. Add milk and stir until thick. Add the browned ground beef and peas, if desired. Heat until warm and serve over toast, rice, or noodles.

Beef Enchiladas

This is one of Rick's favorites.

1 ½ c. cooked shredded beef
1 ½ c. shredded sharp Cheddar cheese, divided
½ c. chopped onion
1 (10¾ oz.) can cream of mushroom soup
1 (10 oz.) can condensed tomato soup
1 (10 oz.) can mild enchilada sauce
12 corn tortillas

Preheat oven to 350°. Combine beef, ½ cup of the cheese and onion; set aside. Combine soups and enchilada sauce. Dip tortillas in hot oil to soften a few seconds on each side. Top each tortilla with 1 heaping tablespoonful of meat mixture; roll up. Place seam side down in 9 x 13-inch baking dish. Pour sauce over tortillas; top with remaining cheese. Bake for 25 to 30 minutes. Refrigerate any leftovers in air-tight container. YIELD: 6 servings.

Nachos

This makes a nice evening snack or a light lunch or supper. Sometimes we'll make these for supper on Sunday nights.

1 lb. ground beef
1 large can refried beans
½ to 1 c. cheese sauce
1 can pitted ripe olives, sliced
guacamole
sour cream
salsa
lettuce (optional)
tomatoes, diced
1 to 2 large bags tortilla chips

Brown ground beef and heat refried beans until warm in saucepan over medium-low heat. Heat cheese sauce as well (or you may use shredded Cheddar cheese and sprinkle it over the layers of beans and beef). Layer refried beans, ground beef, cheese sauce, guacamole, sour cream, and salsa on large plate or platter. Sprinkle with olives, tomatoes, and lettuce, if desired. Arrange tortilla chips around layers. Serve immediately.

Note: I buy "Baker's & Chef's" brand cheese sauce at Sam's Club. It comes in large cans of both Cheddar and nacho cheese flavors.

Tostadas

Easy to make and well-liked.

Brown ground beef with 1 Tbsp. taco seasoning mix. Drain. Heat a can of refried beans. Grate cheese; dice onions and tomatoes. Slice ripe pitted olives. Cut up lettuce. Serve with warmed tostada shells. Everyone can "build" their own.

Tacos

This is an easy meal we serve often. Goes together fast.

2 lb. ground beef
1 pkg. taco flavoring
cheese
tomatoes
onions
lettuce
flour tortillas

Brown ground beef with taco flavoring. Drain, Grate cheese, dice tomatoes, onions, and cut up lettuce. Serve with warm flour tortillas.

Taco Salad

This is a fast, easy favorite. A good meal to serve when Mom and Dad go out to eat, with easy preparation and cleanup! It's one of our son Matt's favorite meals.

2 lb. ground beef
1 chopped onion
1 pkg. taco seasoning mix
2 heads lettuce
1 lb. Cheddar cheese
1 can black olives
4 tomatoes

Brown ground beef with onion and seasoning mix. Drain and cool. Chop lettuce. Grate cheese. Dice tomatoes. Toss all ingredients together. Serve on taco chips with Ranch dressing.

Baked Spaghetti

Another one of our Wednesday night favorites.

½ to 1 c. chopped onion
1 c. chopped green pepper (optional)
1 Tbsp. butter or margarine
1 (28 oz.) can tomatoes with liquid, cut up
1 (4 oz.) can mushroom stems and pieces, drained
1 (2¼ oz.) can sliced ripe olives, drained
2 tsp. dried oregano
1 lb. ground beef, browned & drained (optional)
12 oz. cooked spaghetti, drained
2 c. (8 oz.) shredded Cheddar cheese
1 (10¾ oz.) can cream of mushroom soup
¼ c. water
¼ c. Parmesan cheese

In a large skillet, sauté onion and green pepper until tender. Add tomatoes, mushrooms, olives, and oregano. Add ground beef. Simmer, uncovered, 10 minutes. Place half the spaghetti in a greased 9 x 13-inch pan. Top with half the vegetable mixture. Sprinkle with 1 cup Cheddar cheese. Repeat layers. Mix soup and water until smooth; pour over casserole. Sprinkle with Parmesan cheese. Bake, uncovered, at 350° for 30 to 35 minutes or until heated through. YIELD: 12 servings.

Quick Baked Spaghetti

Fast and easy for a night when you don't have much time for prep.

1 to 2 lb. ground beef
1 lb. spaghetti
1 tall can spaghetti sauce
1 c. sliced ripe olives
2 c. shredded Mozzarella cheese

Brown beef; drain. Add spaghetti sauce; simmer. Meanwhile, cook spaghetti according to package directions. Drain. Combine spaghetti and sauce; turn into a greased 9 x 13-inch baking pan. Top with shredded cheese and olives. Bake at 350° (or 375° if you're in a hurry) until heated through. YIELD: 12 servings.

Stuffed Shells

This is really tasty, and the kids love to help stuff the shells.

Filling:

2 slightly beaten egg whites
1¾ c. cottage or Ricotta cheese
1 c. shredded part skim Mozzarella cheese
2 Tbsp. snipped parsley
1 Tbsp. grated Parmesan cheese
½ tsp. dried Italian seasoning, crushed
¼ tsp. salt
¼ tsp. pepper

Sauce:

1 ½ lb. ground beef
1 large jar spaghetti sauce

Brown ground beef; drain. Add spaghetti sauce and heat through. Cook **16 oz. pkg. large pasta shells** until tender. Stuff with filling. Arrange in 9 x 13-inch pan. Pour sauce evenly over top. Sprinkle grated Mozzarella cheese over sauce. Bake at 350° for 35 to 40 minutes.

Chicken Noodle Casserole

1 (10 oz.) pkg. noodles
1 can cream of chicken soup
1 ½ c. chicken broth
2 to 3 c. cooked chicken, cubed
1 c. Cheddar or Mozzarella cheese, shredded
French fried onions (optional)

Cook noodles according to package directions; drain. Add soup, chicken, and broth. Sprinkle with cheese and top with onions, if desired. Bake at 350° for 30 minutes or until cheese melts and casserole is heated through.

Chicken 'n' Rice Casserole

This is great for company, Sunday dinner, or just anytime!

1 ½ c. uncooked long grain rice
1 can cream of mushroom soup
2 c. water
1 can (1⅔ c.) evaporated milk
1 pkg. onion soup mix
10 pieces chicken

Pour rice in the bottom of a 9 x 13-inch baking dish. Add soup, mixed with water. Add milk and onion soup mix. Place chicken on top. Bake at 350° for an hour. YIELD: 10 servings.

Quick 'n' Easy Barbecued Chicken

1 (18 oz.) bottle barbecue sauce (any flavor)
1 (3 to 3 ½ lb.) whole fryer

Place chicken pieces in 9 x 13-inch baking dish. Cover with sauce and bake 1 hour or until chicken is tender and no longer pink at 350°.

Grilled Chicken Salad

This is a favorite of all. It's a good meal for the kids when Mom and Dad have a night out.

2 heads lettuce, chopped
2 to 3 carrots, sliced
2 cucumbers, sliced
1 to 2 tomatoes, diced
1 c. grated cheese
grilled chicken breasts, diced
hard-boiled eggs (optional)

Combine all ingredients and serve as a main dish or side dish.

Chicken Stuffing Casserole

2 c. cooked chicken or turkey
1 can cream of mushroom soup
2 c. chicken broth
1 can cream of celery soup
1 pkg. cornbread stuffing mix

Place chicken in the bottom of a greased casserole dish; mix soups together and spread on top of chicken. Pour dry stuffing mix on top of soups and pour 2 cups chicken broth over all. Bake at 350° for 30 minutes. YIELD: 6 to 8 servings.

Baked Almond Chicken

This is always my pick for Mother's Day every year. It's kind of rich, but oh, so good! I think it's one of those meals EVERYONE in the family really likes.

½ cup all-purpose flour
⅓ cup plus 1 tbsp. butter, melted, divided
1 tsp paprika
½ tsp. salt
½ tsp. dried oregano
¼ tsp. pepper
6 boneless skinless chicken breast halves
1 ½ cups heavy whipping cream
⅓ cup dry bread crumbs
¾ cup sliced almonds, toasted
Hot cooked pasta (optional)

Place flour in a shallow bowl. Combine ⅓ cup butter and seasonings in another bowl. Coat chicken with flour, then dip in butter mixture. Arrange in a greased shallow 3-quart baking dish. Pour cream around chicken.

Bake, uncovered, at 350° for 45 minutes. Combine bread crumbs and remaining butter; sprinkle over chicken. Top with almonds. Bake, uncovered, for 5-8 minutes or until golden brown. Serve over pasta if desired. YIELD: 6 servings.

Note: We often make it for a special dinner, but not with pasta. Sometimes we make twice baked potatoes and veggies.

Easy Chicken Casserole

1 (10¾ oz.) can cream of chicken soup
1 c. milk
⅛ tsp. salt
dash of white pepper
1 (4 oz.) can mushroom pieces and stems, drained
1 (10 oz.) pkg. or 1 ½ c. frozen mixed vegetables
3 c. diced, cooked chicken or turkey
3 c. corn flakes, crushed to 1½ c.
½ tsp. ground thyme
2 Tbsp. butter or margarine, melted

Butter shallow 2-quart casserole. In large bowl, blend together soup, milk, salt, and pepper. Add mushrooms, cooked vegetables, and chicken; mix well. Turn into casserole. Combine crumbs, thyme, and butter. Sprinkle over top. Bake in 350° oven about 35 minutes or until browned and bubbly. YIELD: 5 to 6 servings.

Broccoli Cheese Chicken

1 Tbsp. margarine or butter
4 skinless, boneless chicken breast halves
1 can broccoli cheese soup
⅓ c. water or milk
2 c. broccoli flowerets
⅛ tsp. pepper

Partially cook and drain frozen vegetables. In skillet over medium heat, in hot margarine or butter, cook chicken 10 minutes or until browned on both sides. Spoon off fat. Stir in remaining ingredients. Heat to boiling. Reduce heat to low. Cover; simmer, stirring occasionally, for 10 minutes or until chicken is tender when tested with fork, and broccoli is done. YIELD: 4 servings.

Cheesy Chicken and Rice

We use this recipe when we have a busy day ahead of us. Pop in the crockpot and you have a delicious supper awaiting you.

Place whole chicken in crockpot. Cover with one can cream of chicken soup and one can Cheddar cheese soup. Cook on low 6 hours or high 4 hours. Serve over rice. Extra good to spoon the sauce over the rice. Easy and delicious.

Roasted Chicken and Brown Gravy

1 tsp. thyme, crushed
¾ tsp. salt
½ tsp. pepper
½ tsp. paprika
1 broiler/fryer, 3 ½ to 4 lbs.
3 bacon strips
¼ c. cold water
1 Tbsp. all-purpose flour

Combine thyme and rosemary, salt, pepper, and paprika. Rub on outside of chicken and inside cavity. Place in shallow roasting pan. Arrange bacon strips over top of chicken. Bake, uncovered, at 450° for 15 minutes. Reduce to 350° for 1 to 1½ hours. Remove chicken from pan. Skim off excess fat from pan juices; combine water and flour and stir into juices. Bring to a boil, stirring constantly. Cook and stir for 1 minute or until thickened. If desired, crumble bacon into gravy. Serve with chicken. YIELD: 4-6 servings.

Chicken Enchiladas

Enchiladas with chicken: they're great! I found this recipe on a soup can years ago and my husband Rick REALLY loves them.

12 corn tortillas
1 chicken, cooked and diced
1 can cream of chicken soup
1 can evaporated milk
1 c. chicken broth
1 lb. grated Cheddar or Velveeta cheese
1 chopped onion
1 can chopped green chilies or 1 (7 ½ oz.) jar taco sauce

Make sauce of soup, milk, chicken broth, and taco sauce. Season with salt and pepper. Place 6 tortillas in bottom of greased 9 x 13-inch pan (cut them in strips if you like). Then add a layer of chicken, onion, and cheese. Add half of the sauce. Repeat layers; top with cheese. Bake at 350° until brown on top, about 45 minutes. YIELD: 12 servings.

Chicken Enchilada Casserole

Good, and good for you!

4 c. uncooked corn tortillas or Fritos corn chips
4 c. cubed, cooked chicken
1 c. All-Bran
1 c. (4 oz.) enchilada sauce
1 (8 oz.) can tomato sauce
⅔ c. (6 oz.) plain low-fat yogurt
4 c. shredded lettuce
⅓ c. sliced green onion
½ c. chopped tomatoes

Combine chicken, All-Bran, cheese, and sauce. Cover with plastic wrap. Microwave on HIGH for 9 minutes, stirring every 3 minutes. Let stand for 5 minutes. Place in serving bowl. Layer yogurt, lettuce, tortilla pieces, green onions, and sauce over casserole. Serve immediately.

Cheese 'n' Chicken Enchiladas

Another yummy enchilada recipe!

1 medium onion
2 Tbsp. margarine
1 ½ c. shredded, cooked chicken
1 (16 oz.) jar picante sauce
1 (3 oz.) pkg. cream cheese, cubed
1 tsp. ground cumin
2 c. extra sharp Cheddar cheese, divided
8 (6-inch) flour tortillas

Heat oven to 350°. Cook and stir onion in margarine until tender. Stir in chicken, ¼ cup picante sauce, cream cheese, and cumin. Heat thoroughly. Stir in 1 cup cheese. Spoon about ⅓ cup chicken mixture in center of each tortilla and roll up. Place seam side down in 12 x 7-inch baking dish. Top with remaining picante sauce and sharp cheese. Bake 15 minutes. YIELD: 8 enchiladas.

Jeremy's Fajitas

A friend's teenager concocted this recipe and it's delicious!

grilled chicken breast meat
garlic salt to taste
mushrooms
grated cheese
flour tortillas
tomatoes
sour cream
avocados (optional)

Sauté chicken with garlic salt in oil. In separate skillet, sauté onions and green peppers in oil. Chop tomatoes. Assemble all ingredients in tortillas and serve with Sweet-and-Sour Sauce, page 26.

Chicken Tetrazzini

This is one of our staple meals. We buy boneless, skinless chicken breasts when they're on sale and freeze them to cook and cube for recipes such as this one.

8 oz. spaghetti, broken in 2-inch pieces
¾ c. canned, sliced mushrooms
4 Tbsp. butter or margarine
3 Tbsp. chopped onion
½ tsp. celery salt or ½ c. chopped celery
1 can cream of mushroom soup
1 can (1⅔ c.) evaporated milk
2 c. cooked chicken or turkey
½ c. sharp Cheddar cheese, grated
½ c. grated Parmesan cheese

Cook spaghetti until tender. Drain and rinse with hot water. Drain mushrooms; reserve liquid. Melt margarine and sauté onion. Add seasoning or celery and mushroom liquid. Blend in soup and stir until smooth. Gradually add milk, stirring constantly, until smooth and thickened. In a 9 x 13-inch pan, mix spaghetti, mushrooms, and chicken. Pour in sauce; mix well. Top with cheeses. Bake at 350° until it bubbles, about 30 minutes. This dish keeps well in refrigerator for a day or so if necessary.

Chicken Fettucine Alfredo

This recipe was made by my daughter Kate at one of our family nights where we ate "Italian" dishes. Everyone loved it and it's easy to make.

5 pieces boneless, skinless chicken
8 oz. uncooked fettucine (we use whole wheat fettucine)

Sauce:

½ c butter or margarine
½ cup heavy whipping cream
¾ c. grated Parmesan cheese
½ tsp. salt
Dash pepper

Bake 5 pieces of boneless skinless chicken at 350° till done, approximately 15-20 minutes. Cut in bite-sized pieces.
Cook fettucine as directed on package. While cooking, make sauce.
Heat butter and whipping cream in 10-inch skillet over medium heat stirring frequently until butter is melted and mixture starts to bubble.
Reduce heat to low, simmer 6 minutes, stirring frequently until slightly thickened. Remove from heat, sprinkle in cheese, salt, and pepper. Drain pasta, pour sauce over it , add cooked chicken, cut in small pieces and sprinkle with parsley.

Chicken and Broccoli Alfredo

½ (8 oz.) pkg. linguine or spaghetti
1 c. fresh or frozen broccoli flowerets
2 Tbsp. butter
1 lb. boneless chicken breasts, cubed
1 (10¾ oz.) can cream of mushroom soup
½ c. milk
½ c. grated Parmesan cheese
¼ tsp. pepper

Cook linguine according to package directions. Add broccoli for the last 4 minutes of cooking time. Drain, Heat butter in skillet. Add chicken and cook until browned, stirring often. Add soup, milk, cheese, pepper, and linguine mixture and heat through. Serve with additional Parmesan cheese. YIELD: 4 servings.

Chicken Delish

1 cut-up fryer
salt and pepper
1 bay leaf, broken up
¼ tsp. oregano or garlic powder
1 can cream of celery soup*
⅔ can evaporated milk

*Cream of chicken or cream of mushroom soup may be substituted for celery.

Place chicken pieces in 9 x 13-inch pan. Add seasonings. Whisk milk and soup until smooth or almost smooth. Pour over chicken. Cover pan with foil. Bake at 350° for 1 hour. Serve by adding cooled rice to the mixture after baking, or pour over cooked rice.

Oven-Fried Chicken

This is a really good alternative to fried chicken. We don't usually fry foods; this is a good way to have the taste without all the work!

1 chicken, cut up
1 c. flour
2 tsp. salt
¼ tsp. pepper
2 tsp. paprika
½ c. margarine

Mix flour, salt, pepper, and paprika in a gallon-size plastic resealable bag. Drop each piece of chicken in bag and shake to coat. Melt margarine in baking pan in 400° oven. Place chicken pieces in pan, turning to coat with margarine. Bake for 45 minutes, then turn and bake until well-browned, 45 minutes more. YIELD: 4 servings.

Chicken or Turkey Divan

Another favorite. I think everyone actually likes this one! We serve it with rice and a yellow vegetable.

2 c. cooked chicken or turkey, diced
1 (10 oz.) pkg. frozen broccoli
6 oz. grated Cheddar cheese
1 (13½ oz.) can evaporated milk
1 (10¾ oz.) can cream of mushroom soup
1 (3½ oz.) can French fried onions

Heat oven to 350°. Arrange chicken in 9 x 13-inch pan. Top with cooked broccoli. Mix liquids together and pour over chicken. Sprinkle with cheese and onions. Bake at 350° for 20 minutes. YIELD: 8 to 10 servings.

Baked Mushroom Chicken with Garlic Butter Pasta

My daughter Kate makes this and it fast became a family night favorite!

Baked Mushroom Chicken:

4 boneless skinless chicken breast halves (1 pound)
¼ c. all-purpose flour
3 Tbsp. butter, divided
1 c. sliced fresh mushrooms
½ c. chicken broth
¼ tsp. salt
⅛ tsp. freshly ground black pepper
⅓ c. shredded mozzarella cheese
⅓ c. grated Parmesan cheese
¼ c. sliced green onions (optional)

Garlic Butter Pasta:

8 oz. spaghetti or linguine
3 Tbsp. olive oil
5 Tbsp. butter, melted
3 garlic cloves, finely chopped
2 Tbsp. chopped, fresh parsley
freshly ground black pepper

Flatten each chicken breast half to ¼-inch thickness. Place flour in a resealable plastic bag; add chicken, a few pieces at a time. Seal and shake to coat. In a large skillet, brown chicken in 2 tablespoons butter on both sides. Transfer to a greased 11 x 2-inch baking dish. In the same skillet, sauté mushrooms in the remaining butter until tender. Add the broth, salt and pepper. Bring to a boil; cook for 5 minutes until liquid is reduced to ½ cup. Spoon over chicken.

Bake, uncovered, at 375° for 15 minutes. Sprinkle with the cheeses and green onions. Bake 5 minutes longer or until the chicken juices run clear.

Meanwhile, cook pasta according to package directions in boiling water to which you have added 1 tablespoon of olive oil; drain thoroughly. Mix together melted butter, garlic and parsley. Stir into the pasta and serve immediately with black pepper and chicken. YIELD: 4 servings.

Chicken and Homemade Noodles

Rick's mom taught me to make this recipe in the early years of our marriage when my oldest boys were just babies. Start the noodles in the morning. This makes a nice supper for a cold winter evening.

Noodles:

1 c. all-purpose flour
3 egg yolks
1 egg
2 tsp. salt
¼ to ½ c. water

1 whole chicken
1 stick celery, cut in pieces, if desired

Measure flour into bowl; make a well in center and add egg yolks, whole egg, and salt. With hands, thoroughly mix egg into flour. Add water, one tablespoon at a time, mixing thoroughly after each addition. (Add only enough water to form dough into a ball.) Turn dough onto a well-floured cloth-covered board; knead until smooth and elastic, about 10 minutes. Cover, let rest 10 minutes.

Divide dough into 4 equal parts. Roll dough, one part at a time, into paper-thin rectangle, keeping remaining dough covered. Roll rectangle around rolling pin; slip out rolling pin. Cut dough crosswise into ⅛-inch strips for narrow noodles and ¼-inch strips for wide noodles. Shake out strips and place on towel to dry, about 2 hours.

Meanwhile, boil the whole chicken with the celery. Cool; pick meat off bones. Save broth.

When noodles are dry, break dry strips into smaller pieces. Add noodles and chicken pieces to broth. Cook until tender, 12 to 15 minutes. Ladle into bowls; serve with fresh bread.

Meat and Rice Casserole

1 ½ c. Minute rice
1 can cream of mushroom soup
2 to 3 slices American or Cheddar cheese
1 c. diced turkey ham*

**Note: You may use chopped hot dogs, chicken, turkey, ham, or other meat of your choice in place of turkey ham, if desired. Grated cheese may be substituted for the slices.*

Cook rice according to package directions. When done, mix in soup and cheese. Heat and stir until cheese melts. Add turkey ham. Turn into casserole dish and bake at 350° until heated thoroughly.
Variation: When rushed for time, simply heat a minute or two longer on the stove and serve.

Calico Beans

A good meal on a cold snowy day. Serve with hot fresh bread or rolls.

2 c. pinto beans, cooked and drained
2 c. Northern beans, cooked and drained
2 c. red kidney beans, cooked and drained
1 qt. pork and beans
1 lb ground beef
1 ½ onions, cut up
¾ c. brown sugar
2 tsp. salt
1 clove minced garlic
½ c. vinegar
½ c. ketchup

Preheat oven to 325°. Combine beans in large casserole, reserving liquids. Fry the ground beef and onions briefly. Add the brown sugar, salt, garlic, vinegar, and ketchup. Cook 5 minutes and pour over beans. Add enough reserved bean liquid to barely cover beans. Bake, uncovered, 1½ hours, adding additional liquid if beans become too dry. YIELD: 10 to 12 servings.

Baked Macaroni and Cheese

My daughter Kate makes this, and it's delicious!

2 Tbsp. butter or margarine
2 Tbsp. flour
1 tsp. salt
1 tsp. dry mustard (optional)*
2 ½ c. milk
2 c. (8 oz.) shredded Cheddar cheese
8 oz. elbow macaroni
¼ c. buttered bread crumbs (optional)*
paprika

**I omit mustard and bread crumbs and increase the amount of cheese on top.*

In saucepan, melt butter. Remove from heat; blend in flour, salt, and mustard. Add milk; heat, stirring constantly until sauce is smooth and begins to thicken. Add 1½ cups cheese and stir until melted.
Meanwhile, cook macaroni as directed. Drain. Combine with sauce in 2-quart saucepan. Top with remaining cheese, bread crumbs, if desired, and paprika. Bake at 375° for 20 to 25 minutes, or until nicely browned and bubbly. YIELD: 4 to 6 servings.

Creamy Baked Macaroni and Cheese

This recipe came from my daughter-in-law, Kari. It's favorite with everyone.

8 oz. macaroni (I like to use whole wheat to boost up the nutrition)
2 Tbsp. butter
2 Tbsp. flour
1 tsp. salt
2 ½ c. milk
2 c. grated sharp cheddar cheese, divided
paprika

Bring water to a boil. Add macaroni, and cook according to your package instructions. Drain. Place in a lightly greased casserole dish (an 8-inch, 11 x 7-inch, or a 2-quart will work fine). Meanwhile, melt the butter in a pot over medium-high heat. Once melted, stir in flour and salt until the flour is fully incorporated with the butter. Add milk. Using a whisk, which will help to break up the clumps, stir almost constantly until the mixture thickens. Add 1½ cups of cheese and stir until melted (and just as a side note, I almost always prefer to use freshly grated cheese. I think it makes a big difference in the texture of the sauce). Now pour all of the sauce over the macaroni and give it a little stir to make sure there is sauce in all the cracks. Sprinkle the remaining ½ cup of cheese over the top. Sprinkle with salt and pepper, to taste. Lightly sprinkle with paprika (optional). Now bake, uncovered, at 375° for about 20-25 minutes, or until bubbly.

Omelets

We often invite a group of friends over on Sunday nights after church and Rick makes custom omelets on our griddle for everyone. We usually serve omelets with biscuits and honey or jelly and choice of orange juice, cranberry juice or milk. It's a lot of fun.

2 to 3 eggs
¼ c. milk
finely chopped ham
grated Cheddar cheese
chopped black olives
chopped onion
chopped tomatoes

Mix the eggs and milk with a wire whisk. Pour onto hot griddle. Add the ham, cheese, black olives, onion, and tomatoes to taste. Fold in half and cook until egg is cooked through. *Delicious!*

Homemade Pizza

4 c. flour
pinch of sugar
1 ½ c. warm water
1 ½ Tbsp. yeast
1 ½ Tbsp. oil
pizza sauce
Mozzarella cheese
optional toppings*

*Optional toppings: Ripe olives, browned hamburger or sausage, ham, pepperoni, bacon, kielbasa, chopped green pepper, mushrooms, and onion.

Dissolve yeast in water. Stir in crust ingredients. Spread in oiled pizza pans. Top with pizza sauce, cheese and your choice of other toppings. Bake at 425° for 10 minutes. (Lift corner of crust with a spatula to test for doneness. When bottom of crust is golden brown, pizza is ready.) YIELD: 4 pizzas.

When my fourth son, Josh, who is now in heaven, was battling leukemia, we came home from an exhausting day at University of Virginia's hospital. My sister and her son were visiting and Josh insisted I make them my homemade pizza. I didn't feel like cooking anything, but he told his cousin Johnny, "Mom makes the best pizza in the world. You've got to try it." It was the last time Josh ever ate Mom's pizza and am I ever glad I mustered up the energy to fix it for him.

Broiled Scrod or Swordfish

Delicious and good for you!

Place fresh scrod or swordfish steak on broiler pan and sprinkle with juice from a lemon. Broil about 7 minutes per side, depending on thickness.

Tuna Casserole

Another old family favorite as I was growing up. This also makes a good lunch.

1 lb. egg noodles
1 to 2 cans cream of mushroom soup
¼ c. milk
1 can drained tuna

Boil the noodles until tender; drain. Add soup, milk, and tuna. Spread in baking dish and top with crushed Ritz crackers or potato chips. Bake 15 minutes at 350°.

Shrimp Wiggle

This was my mom's recipe. She lived on Cape Cod and we often had fresh seafood. This was one of our favorites and still is with some of my kids. This also makes a great Saturday night meal or a special lunch.

1 stick butter
8 Tbsp. flour
3 c. milk
2 c. frozen shrimp, thawed

Melt butter in saucepan. Add flour and stir out lumps. Add milk and stir until thick and smooth. Add shrimp. Stir over low heat until heated through. Serve over toast, noodles, or rice.

Garden Lunch

In summer we often steam vegetables from the garden or store, including cabbage, summer squash, broccoli, and cauliflower. Serve with butter, salt, and cheese, if desired. We usually serve sliced cucumbers and Ranch salad dressing to dip them in.

Country Brunch Skillet

6 bacon strips
6 c. frozen cubed hash brown potatoes
¾ c. chopped green pepper (optional)
½ c. chopped onion
1 tsp. salt
¼ tsp. pepper
6 eggs
½ c. shredded Cheddar cheese

In large skillet over medium heat, cook bacon until crisp. Remove bacon; crumble and set aside. Drain, reserving 2 tablespoons of drippings. Add potatoes, green pepper, onion, salt, and pepper to drippings; cook and stir for 2 minutes. Cover and cook, stirring occasionally, until potatoes are browned and tender, about 15 minutes. Make 6 wells in the potato mixture; break 1 egg into each well. Cover and cook over low heat for 6 to 8 minutes or until eggs are completely set. Sprinkle with cheese and bacon. YIELD: 6 servings.

Stuffed Tomatoes

I learned how to make these from my Mom. We always had a garden growing up and this is a fantastic way to use tomatoes. Nothing like a home grown tomato! An easy lunch!

fresh tomatoes
tuna
mayonnaise or salad dressing

Wash tomatoes. Combine tuna (drained) and mayonnaise. Onions and celery may be added if desired. Core tomatoes; slice from top to halfway through 4 times to make 8 flower-like petals. Fill with tuna salad. Egg salad may also be used. Serve immediately.

"Layer Supper"

This we first had at a Mennonite friend's house. It's quite nutritious, easy to fix, and the kids loved making their own layers and pouring on the sauce. An easy, nutritious dish.

Cook a bowl of brown rice, a bowl of pinto beans, and a bowl of peas (canned peas may be used). For each plate, layer a serving of beans, then peas, then rice. Spoon Cheese Sauce over top. *continued on page 60*

"LAYER SUPPER" *continued*

Cheese Sauce:

1 stick margarine
8 Tbsp. flour
2 c. milk
2 c. grated cheese

Melt margarine in saucepan. Add flour. Add milk and stir until thick. Add cheese. Cook over low or medium-low heat until cheese is melted and sauce is thick.

STROMBOLIS

A Saturday night special. We tried to duplicate a restaurant's strombolis. My 10-year-old loves to make these for supper all by herself!

Thaw 1 package frozen bread dough or make your own pizza dough. Roll out in circle on greased or floured countertop. Spread on one-half of the circle: pepperoni, grated Mozzarella cheese, slices of Provolone cheese, sliced black olives, Canadian bacon, if desired, and chopped canned mushrooms. Sprinkle with Molly McButter roasted garlic seasoning. Fold top of circle down over ingredients and pinch shut around edges, forming a semi-circle. Place on greased cookie sheet. Bake at 425° for about 15 minutes or until lightly browned. Serve with heated pizza sauce for dipping.

HOAGIES

Another recipe developed by trying to imitate the one in a restaurant. They're a real favorite with everyone and they're fast and easy to prepare.

I use whole wheat hoagie buns. Sauté sliced onions in margarine until tender. Drain and set aside. I use Steak-umm sandwich steaks. I cook them on a griddle (I use a large one, so I can cook a lot at once). They cook really fast. As soon as I flip them over to cook on the second side, I sprinkle grated Mozzarella cheese on half of each. When melted, fold over lengthwise. Place on bun. Spread with mayonnaise, ketchup, mustard, and relish to suit your tastes.

Bacon-Broccoli Quiche p. 69

Sweet Potato Casserole p. 63

Twice-Baked Potatoes p. 65

Vegetables

Vegetables

Mozzarella Zucchini Skillet

In summer, we usually have an overabundance of zucchini. My mom made up this recipe and it's delicious.

Slice zucchini in skillet. Cover with tomato sauce; season with salt, pepper, and oregano. Simmer until tender. Sprinkle grated Mozzarella on top until melted.

Corn Pudding

2 cans of corn, drained
6 Tbsp. margarine, melted
6 tsp. flour
2 c. sugar
3 c. milk
6 eggs
2 tsp. vanilla
cinnamon
nutmeg

Lightly grease a 9 x13-inch dish. Put in the corn and add the flour and margarine. Mix well and spread evenly in pan. In separate bowl, mix together the sugar, milk, vanilla, and cinnamon. Add the eggs and mix well. Pour over the corn mixture. Bake at 450° for 40 to 45 minutes. If desired, add some nutmeg after baking for 25 minutes.
Recipe can be doubled using two 9 x 13-inch pans.

Squash Casserole

Wonderful, especially if you grow your own squash.

3 lb. chopped, cooked yellow squash, drained, or 2-qt. canned squash, drained
½ c. chopped onion
½ c. yellow cornmeal
½ c. melted margarine or butter
2 eggs, beaten
1 Tbsp. sugar
1 tsp. salt
¼ tsp. pepper

Mash squash; add onion, half of cornmeal, and half of margarine. Mix well. Add eggs, sugar, salt, and pepper. Pour into slightly greased or buttered baking dish and lightly sprinkle with remaining cornmeal. Slowly drizzle remainder of butter across top. Bake in oven at 375° approximately 1 hour. YIELD: 8 servings.

Scalloped Potatoes

6 to 8 medium potatoes
6 Tbsp. margarine or butter
6 Tbsp. flour
1 ½ tsp. salt
½ tsp. pepper
3 c. milk
¼ c. minced onion
2 c. sharp Cheddar cheese, grated

Peel potatoes and cut into thin slices. Cover with water and boil for 5 minutes. Drain and pour into a 2-quart casserole. Melt margarine in saucepan. Stir in flour and seasonings. Add milk slowly. Add onion and cheese. Cook and stir over medium heat until boiling. Pour over potatoes. Sprinkle with more grated cheese. Bake at 350° for 30 to 45 minutes. YIELD: 8 servings.

Sweet Potato Casserole

This is one of our very favorite dishes for Thanksgiving dinner. My daughter Kate loves to make this dish.

3 cups sweet potatoes, mashed
1 stick margarine or butter
2 eggs
1 c. sugar
1 Tbsp. vanilla

Use mixer and mix all ingredients. Pour into 9 x13-inch pan.

Sprinkle on top:

1 c. brown sugar
⅓ c. butter or margarine
⅓ c. flour

Work together with fork, pat with fingers and sprinkle **1 cup pecans** on top. Bake at 350° for 1 hour.

Cheesy Potatoes

Got this recipe from my mother-in-law. Very tasty.

Cook potatoes. Cut up into casserole dish. Mix a can of Cheddar cheese soup with ½ can milk. Heat and stir until smooth. Pour over potatoes and stir until potatoes are coated. Crush potato chips; sprinkle over potatoes for topping. Bake at 350° until heated through.
Optional: You may also cook these on the stove and potato chip topping may be omitted according to preference.

Potato Casserole

2 lb. frozen hash browns
¾ c. melted butter, divided
1 tsp. salt
¼ tsp. pepper
½ c. chopped onion
1 can cream of mushroom soup
1 pt. sour cream
2 c. shredded Cheddar cheese
2 c. crushed corn flakes

Defrost potatoes. In a large bowl, combine potatoes, salt, pepper, onion, soup, ½ cup of the butter, sour cream and cheese. Place in a 3-quart casserole dish. Mix remaining butter and corn flakes. Sprinkle over potato mixture. Bake at 350° for 35 minutes. YIELD: 12 servings.
To prepare ahead of time, cover with foil and store in refrigerator. Allow more time to bake if cold.

Twice Baked Potatoes

I always request these for my birthday supper. Worth the extra effort and you can bake the potatoes ahead of time.

6 medium-large baking potatoes
2-3 Tbsp. sour cream
1 Tbsp. butter
Salt to taste
Pinch of pepper
½ cup milk
¾ cup Cheddar cheese, grated
½ cup bacon bits

Bake 6 baking potatoes in their skins till tender. Let them cool briefly. Cut lengthwise and scoop out centers. Place skins in a baking dish. Put scooped out potatoes in bowl.
Mash potatoes in bowl with milk, sour cream, salt and pepper, and butter. Scoop the mixture back into potato skins. Sprinkle with cheese and bacon bits and bake at 350° for 15 minutes or until heated through. Delicious!
YIELD: 12 servings.

Variation: Add 3 Tbsp. ranch dressing in place of the sour cream

Cheese Potato Puff

12 medium potatoes, peeled and cubed
2 c. (8 oz.) shredded Cheddar or Swiss cheese, divided
1¼ c. milk
½ c. butter or margarine, softened
1 to 2 tsp. salt
2 eggs, beaten

Place the potatoes in a saucepan and cover with water; cover and bring to a boil. Cook until tender, about 15 to 20 minutes. Drain and mash. Add 1¾ cups cheese, milk, butter, and salt; cook and stir over low heat until the cheese and butter are melted. Fold in eggs. Spread into a greased 9 x 13 x 2-inch baking dish. Bake, uncovered, at 350° for 25 to 20 minutes. Sprinkle with the remaining cheese. Bake 5 minutes longer or until golden brown.
YIELD: 12 to 14 servings.

Cheese Fries

Use frozen French fries from the store. Bake according to package directions. During the last 5 minutes of cooking, sprinkle with shredded Cheddar cheese and bacon bits. Serve with Ranch dressing.

Oven-Fried Potatoes

6 to 8 large potatoes, cut in half 4 times
½ c. vegetable oil
2 Tbsp. grated Parmesan cheese
¼ tsp. garlic powder
½ tsp. paprika

Lay potato strips in single layer on deep baking sheet. Add Parmesan cheese, garlic powder, and paprika to the oil. Stir; pour over potatoes. Bake at 425° for 30 to 45 minutes or until tender.
Variation*:* Use half or all sweet potatoes. We have a large garden and grow sweet potatoes every year. This is a recipe we have often.

Baked Potatoes Supreme

We often bake potatoes as a main dish for lunch and serve with a variety of toppings.

baked potatoes
bacon bits
grated cheese or cheese sauce
broccoli
diced hard-boiled eggs
sour cream
salsa

Choose any or all of above.

Chinese Fried Rice

4 to 6 c. cooked rice
1 small head cabbage
6 to 8 fresh mushrooms or small jar of canned
1 (8 oz.) bag chipped beef, chopped
6 to 10 green onions, chopped
½ c. celery
3 to 4 eggs
2 tsp. garlic powder
2 Tbsp. soy sauce

Beat eggs, garlic powder, and soy sauce together. Set aside. Heat oil; add chopped garlic and green onions. Cook until translucent. Add beef, mushrooms, celery, and then cabbage. Add eggs and onions, then add cooked rice. Toss it until hot, then add soy sauce to taste. Serve warm.

Fried Rice

This is my daughter-in-law Christina's recipe. Very tasty! It's a very handy recipe if you have small amounts of leftover meat and/or veggies. When I make rice, I usually make enough to last for a few meals. Then if we have leftovers later, I will use the rice and leftovers to make fried rice.

1 c. cooked meat, diced (chicken, steak, ham, pork chops, shrimp, etc.)
1 c. frozen corn
1 c. frozen peas
½ c. sliced green onions or finely diced purple onion*
2 eggs, scrambled and crumbled into similar size pieces as peas/corn/meat
4 c. cooked non-instant rice
3 Tbsp. oil or butter
garlic salt to taste
pepper to taste
Maggi brand sauce or soy sauce, to taste

In large skillet or pot, add rice and butter or oil. Stir and cook over medium or high heat until rice is no longer lumpy.

*If using purple onion, add to rice now and mix well. This gives the onion a longer time to cook, resulting in a milder flavor.

Push rice to the edges of pot or skillet, leaving an empty area in the middle. Add frozen peas and corn into the middle, stirring in the middle until peas and corn are heated through. (This saves having to cook the peas and corn separately.) Add meat, scrambled eggs and green onion. Stir entire contents. Add garlic salt, pepper, and Maggi sauce/soy sauce to taste.

You may cook this entree entirely in one skillet/pot, even if you do not have scrambled eggs already made. Just mix the raw eggs, and cook them in the skillet/pot with some oil or butter, stirring constantly until thoroughly cooked and crumbled. Then add the rice and continue from beginning. Mixed frozen veggies may be substituted for frozen peas and corn.

Baked Beans

family size can pork and beans
½ c. ketchup
1 c. brown sugar
1 small onion, chopped
3 strips bacon

Combine all ingredients and pour into a 9 x 13-inch pan. Cover with aluminum foil, then poke holes in it. Bake 1½ hours at 350°, or if you're in a hurry, 45 minutes to 1 hour at 425°.

French Fried Green Beans

2 cans green beans
1 can cream of mushroom soup
⅓ c. milk
1 large can French fried onions, divided
salt and pepper to taste

Mix half the can of onions with all other ingredients. Transfer to a 2-quart casserole. Bake at 350° for 20 minutes. Sprinkle remaining onions on top. Bake 5 minutes more. YIELD: 6 to 8 servings.

Broccoli Casserole

1 (10 oz.) pkg. frozen chopped broccoli
1 egg, beaten
¼ c. milk
½ c. mayonnaise
1 can cream of mushroom soup
buttered cracker crumbs
1 c. shredded Cheddar cheese

Cook broccoli in lightly salted water; drain. Combine egg, milk, soup, mayonnaise, and cheese. Stir in cooked broccoli. Pour into greased 1-quart dish. Sprinkle with cracker crumbs. Bake at 350° for 30 minutes. Let cool 15 minutes before serving.

Corn State Broccoli Bake

This recipe my daughter got from Taste of Home website. Excellent.

1 package (8 oz.) Chicken in a Biskit crackers, crushed
½ cup butter, melted
3 cups frozen chopped broccoli, thawed
1 can (15¼ oz.) whole kernel corn, drained
1 can (14¾ oz.) cream-style corn

Combine cracker crumbs and butter; reserve ½ cup for topping. In a bowl, combine broccoli, both cans of corn, and remaining crumbs. Transfer to a greased 2-qt. baking dish. Sprinkle with reserved crumb mixture. Bake, uncovered, at 375° for 25-30 minutes or until lightly browned. YIELD: 6 t0 8 servings.

Bacon and Broccoli Quiche

Laura makes this and it so good.

2 cups flour
½ tsp. salt
¾ cup butter or shortening
3-4 Tbsp. water (cold)
4 eggs
12 bacon strips, cooled and crumbed
 or 1 roll sausage, cooked
1 c. broccoli, cooked
2 c. milk
¼ tsp. salt
¼ tsp pepper
Garlic powder
Onion powder
1¼ cup shredded cheese

Combine flour and salt in a bowl. Cut in butter/shortening with pastry blender until mixture resembles coarse crumbs. Add water, a little at a time, until dough comes away from bowl. Form into a ball. Divide ball in half and freeze half. Roll other half to fit a 9 in. pie plate. Trim and flute edges. Chill. For filling: Beat eggs, milk and seasonings. Stir in cheese and bacon or sausage. Pour into crust. Bake at 425° for 15 minutes. Reduce temperature to 325°. Continue to bake for 30-40 minutes or until knife inserted in center comes out clean.

Steamed Cauliflower with Cheese Sauce

We often have this for lunch in the summertime, or as a side dish for dinner.

2 heads fresh cauliflower, rinsed well
½ c. butter or margarine
8 Tbsp. all-purpose flour
1 tsp. salt
¼ tsp. pepper
3 ½ c. milk
2 to 3 c. shredded Cheddar cheese

Separate cauliflower florets. Place in a steamer pan and cook on high until tender. Reduce heat to low. Meanwhile, melt butter or margarine. Add flour, salt, and pepper; stir until smooth. Slowly add milk, stirring over medium-low heat. Cook until mixture is smooth and begins to thicken a little. Add cheese; heat, stirring constantly, until sauce is thick and smooth. Serve hot with cauliflower.

Toll House Pie p. 96

Parmesan Yeast Rolls p. 75

Basic Sandwich Bread p. 73

Breads, Rolls & Pastries

Breads, Rolls & Pastries

Whole Wheat Bread

11 c. whole-wheat flour
1 Tbsp. dough enhancer
3 ½ c. water
⅓ c. oil
⅓ c. honey
1 ½ Tbsp. yeast

Mix water and several cups flour. Knead briefly. Add honey, yeast, and oil. Let knead 6 to 8 minutes. (When dough pulls away from the side of the bowl, you have enough flour.) Oil the counter. Shape bread into loaves. Place in pans and let rise 25 minutes. Bake for 20 minutes at 350°. YIELD: 5 loaves.

Light Wheat Bread

This used to be the basic recipe that I used most often. It's quick and easy to make, and light for a 100% whole wheat bread.

12 c. whole-wheat flour
4 ½ c. warm water
½ c. oil
½ c. honey
1 Tbsp. salt
1 Tbsp. dough enhancer (optional, but nice)
2 Tbsp. Wheat gluten (optional, but nice)

With Bosch or KitchenAid stand mixer, mix water, oil, honey, salt, and wheat gluten for about a minute. Add 6 cups whole-wheat flour. Add 3 tablespoons yeast to ½ cup whole-wheat flour and add to mixture. Continue to add more flour, one cup at a time, until dough pulls away from sides (about 5 to 6 more cups). Knead 10 minutes.
Wet counter with water; also wet hands and rolling pin. Divide dough into 5 sections. Now you choose—plain, cinnamon, sweet rolls, etc. Roll dough flat. For cinnamon bread, drizzle with honey and sprinkle with cinnamon. Spread with a fork. Roll dough to form a log. Roll edges in. Place in pan, poke with a fork. Sprinkle lightly with cinnamon. Let bread rise in a warm oven for 30 to 40 minutes.
Turn oven up to 325° and bake 20 to 25 minutes. Let cool 5 to 10 minutes and turn out onto its side to cool. YIELD: 5 loaves.

For sweet rolls:

When rolling out dough, roll flat; sprinkle with cinnamon and spread with honey. Roll into log, and then cut into 12 equal pieces. Place in pan to rise. Follow directions above. Glaze with a confectioner's sugar glaze after baking.

Basic Sandwich Bread

My daughter Christa makes us all this delicious whole wheat bread with freshly ground white winter wheat. It's our staple. We eat it almost every day. Very light and with the freshly ground whole wheat, it has a mild flavor. She usually makes several batches at a time, cools and then cuts into slices and freezes. When we want to use it we just take out the desired amount of slices. We use it for sandwiches or I love to use it for toast spread with peanut butter and jam. Also makes great cheese bread or garlic bread to use with a pasta meal.

2 c. hot water
⅓ c. oil
⅓ c. honey
1 egg
3 ½ tsp. instant yeast
5 c. whole wheat flour
2 tsp. salt
1-2 Tbsp. lecithan (optional)
1 tsp. gluten (optional)

Combine water. oil and honey.
Add 3 cups flour, yeast, salt, lecithin, and gluten. Mix thoroughly. Add egg and mix. Add the remaining flour and knead (I use a mixer with dough hook) until smooth and elastic about 10 minutes. Place in greased bowl and let rise until doubled. Shape into two loaves or dinner rolls and let rise again for about ½ hour to 1 hour. Bake at 350° for 20-30 minutes until lightly browned.

Swedish Bread

This is my mom's recipe. We had Swedish bread every Christmas and Easter morning. Did we ever look forward to it! Mom would shape the dough into braids and top with maraschino cherries. Yummy!

2 ½ c. scalded milk
1 yeast cake (1 Tbsp.)
flour (about 7 c.)
½ c. melted butter
⅔ c. sugar
1 egg, well beaten
½ tsp. salt
1 tsp. almond extract
5-6 cardamom seeds, crushed (optional)

Dissolve yeast cake in ½ cup milk which has been allowed to cool until lukewarm. Add ½ cup flour; beat thoroughly. Cover and let rise. When light, stir in remaining milk and 4½ cups flour. Stir until well mixed. Cover and let rise; then add remaining ingredients and 1½ cups flour. Turn onto floured cloth and knead using ½ cup flour. Cover again and let rise. Shape and rise. Bake 20 minutes at 350°.

Cardamom Braids

1 pkg. active dry yeast
1 ½ c. warm milk (110° to 115°), divided
1 c. sugar, divided
3 egg yolks, beaten
½ tsp. salt
½ c. butter or margarine, softened
1 Tbsp. ground cardamom
5 to 6 c. all-purpose flour
2 Tbsp. milk

In a large mixing bowl, dissolve yeast in ½ cup warm milk. Add ¼ cup sugar, egg yolks, butter, cardamom, salt, 3 cups of flour and remaining warm milk; beat until smooth. Stir in enough remaining flour to form a soft dough. Turn onto a floured surface; knead until smooth and elastic, about 6 to 8 minutes. Place in a greased bowl, turning once to grease top. Cover and let rise in a warm place until doubled, about 1¼ hours.

Punch dough down; divide into 6 pieces. Shape each piece into a 16-inch rope. Place 3 ropes on a greased baking sheet; braid. Pinch ends firmly and tuck under. Repeat with remaining 3 ropes on another baking sheet. Cover and let rise until doubled, about 45 minutes. Brush braids with milk and sprinkle with remaining sugar. Bake at 350° for 25 to 30 minutes or until golden brown. Remove to wire racks to cool. YIELD: 2 loaves.

Butternut Squash Rolls

This was another of my mom's recipes. We always grew butternut squash. This makes light, delicious rolls!

½ c. cooled, strained butternut squash
¼ c. sugar
½ tsp. salt
½ c. milk
¼ yeast cake
¼ c. lukewarm water
¼ c. butter
2½ c. flour

Dissolve yeast in water; mix in other ingredients and let rise until light. Shape in muffin pans, clover leaf style. Bake at 375° for 15-20 minutes or until lightly browned.

Parmesan Yeast Rolls

My daughter Carrie makes these for family nights. They are so good!

2 c. water
1 Tbsp. and 2 tsp. yeast
½ c. sugar
¼ c. oil
1 egg
2 tsp. lecithin, optional
5-6 cups freshly ground whole wheat flour
4 Tbsp. butter
6 Tbsp. Parmesan
1-2 tsp. garlic to taste

Dissolve yeast in warm water in mixing bowl. In a large bowl mix together the sugar, oil, egg, and lecithin. Add yeast/water and mix. Add flour cup by cup until dough is workable but not too stiff. Knead for 6 minutes. Place in greased bowl, covered loosely with plastic wrap or a kitchen towel and let rise until doubled, approximately 1 hour. Roll dough up into 24 balls. place in greased muffin tins. let rise again approximately ½ hour. Bake at 350° for 14-17 minutes.

For topping: Melt butter. Add Parmesan and garlic powder. Stir until thoroughly combined. Brush over baked rolls.

Note: dough is very versatile—I use for cinnamon rolls, pizza dough, etc.

Pepperoni Rolls

1⅓ c. warm water
1 ½ tsp. yeast
1 ½ tsp salt
2 Tbsp. sugar
2 Tbsp. oil
3 ½ c. whole wheat flour

Place warm water in bowl. Sprinkle in yeast, stirring constantly till dissolved. Add salt, sugar, oil and then slowly add flour stirring constantly. Let rise in warm place till doubled, approximately 1 hour. Shape into roll-sized pieces and place several pieces of pepperoni and 2 Tbsp. Mozzarella cheese in center of each roll. Pinch edges together forming a ball. Melt margarine and brush on top of rolls. Sprinkle on top of each, a mixture of 1½ tsp. basil, 1 tsp parsley, garlic powder to taste, and ⅓ cup Parmesan cheese. Bake at 400° till lightly browned, approximately 12 minutes. Dip in pizza sauce.

Winter Squash Rolls

1 c. milk
1 c. water
½ brown sugar
1 ½ tsp. salt
4 Tbsp. butter, softened
1 pkg. yeast
¼ c. lukewarm water
¼ tsp. sugar
1 whole egg
2 egg yolks
1 c. squash, pureed
1 tsp. lemon peel or rind, grated
8 c. flour

Preheat oven to 375°. In separate saucepans, scald milk and bring water to a boil. Place brown sugar and salt into large mixing bowl. Stir in milk and water until butter is melted; cool to lukewarm. Sprinkle yeast over ¼ cup lukewarm water; add sugar and allow to dissolve 10 minutes. Beat whole egg and yolks lightly with fork and stir unto milk/butter/sugar mixture. Add yeast mixture, squash, and lemon rind and combine thoroughly. Add enough of the flour, ½ cup at a time, to make a soft, sticky dough that comes clean from sides of bowl. Cover, let rise 1½ hours or until doubled. Punch down. Lightly butter hands and pinch off egg-shaped pieces of dough, placing in buttered 3-inch muffin cups. Cover, allow to rise 30 minutes or until doubled. Bake for 15 to 20 minutes. YIELD: 2 dozen rolls.

To make into bread:

Arrange egg-sized pieces side by side into 2 buttered loaves. Let rise 45 minutes. Bake 45 to 55 minutes. Slice or pull apart and serve as rolls. YIELD: 2 loaves.

Butterhorns

An old North Dakota farm recipe. I make these for breakfast on Christmas mornings.

2 pkg. yeast
1 tsp. sugar
6 eggs, well beaten
1 c. sugar
1 tsp. salt
1 c. melted lard or oil
2 c. lukewarm milk
9 c. flour (approximately)

Soak yeast and sugar in a little warm water. Combine all ingredients, using enough flour to make a soft dough. Let stand until doubled. Take part of dough and roll into round like a pie crust, only about ⅓ inch thick. Cut in pie-like wedges and brush with melted butter. Roll each wedge, starting with large end and pinching the point underneath. Bake 18 minutes at 350°. Glaze while still hot.

Glaze:

2 c. powdered sugar
2 tsp. milk

Add milk or water, little by little, until the right consistency is reached.

One-Hour Yeast Rolls

These are quick to whip up and my family loves them! They disappear immediately. Great for company, too.

⅔ c. boiling water
3 Tbsp. shortening or margarine
2 Tbsp. sugar
1 tsp. salt
1 pkg. dry yeast
1 beaten egg
2 c. flour

Melt shortening or margarine in boiling water. Add sugar and salt. When slightly cool, add yeast and 1 beaten egg and beat in flour. Beat well. Let rise in a warm place for 30 minutes. Roll dough out in a circle on a floured board and spread with melted butter. Cut into 12 pie-shaped wedges. Roll up in crescents and let rise another 30 minutes. Bake at 400° for 15 minutes. YIELD: 1 dozen.

Chrissy's Cinnamon Rolls

These are a favorite with the whole family any time of the year, but when we take our yearly beach trip, the grandkids always request that Aunt Christa make her cinnamon rolls to bring for a yummy breakfast. Good and good for you.

Dough:

1 Tbsp. yeast
⅓ c. sugar
1 tsp. salt
4 c. flour (We use freshly ground whole wheat flour)
1 c. warm water
½ c. butter
2 eggs

Dissolve yeast, sugar and salt in warm water. Add soft butter. eggs, and flour, mix well. Knead for 8 minutes (I use a mixer with dough hook.) Let rise in greased bowl until doubled. Roll out on floured surface. spread with soft butter and then coat with cinnamon mixture and press in gently. Roll into log and then slice into 1-inch rolls. Bake at 400° for 10 minutes. Cool slightly and then ice with cream cheese icing. They melt in your mouth.

Cinnamon mixture:

¼ c. soft butter
1 c. brown sugar
3 Tbsp. cinnamon

Mix cinnamon and sugar together. Pour over buttered dough.

Icing:

½ c. soft butter
1 ½ c. powdered sugar
2 oz. cream cheese
2 Tbsp. half and half
1 tsp. vanilla
pinch of salt

Cream butter and cream cheese. Add vanilla, salt, powdered sugar and enough half and half to reach desired consistency.

Oatmeal Rolls or Bread

Every Saturday night growing up, we had Mom's oatmeal rolls. Delicious! Makes my mouth water to think of them!

1 ½ c. boiling water
1 c. rolled oats
1 tsp. salt
⅓ c. honey
1 ½ tsp. oil
1 Tbsp. yeast
¼ c. water
3 ½ c. flour (½ whole-wheat, if desired)

Pour boiling water over oatmeal. Add salt; stir and cool. Dissolve the yeast in warm water. Add to the oats. Add honey and oil. Gradually stir in flour. Knead for 5 minutes. Place in buttered bowl and allow to rise until doubled, about 1 hour.

Then punch down and pat into a greased loaf pan or break off small pieces of dough to form 1-inch balls and place in two 9-inch cake pans. Let rise another hour. Bake bread at 375° for 50 minutes. Bake rolls at 375° for 20 minutes.

Anadama Bread

This is another one of my mom's recipes and my very favorite of all. A delicious blend of flavor!

1¾ c. water
½ c. oatmeal
2 tsp. salt
½ c. molasses
2 Tbsp. shortening
1 pkg. yeast (1 Tbsp.)
½ c. warm water
4 to 5 c. flour

Combine water, cornmeal, and salt in pan. Bring to a boil, stirring constantly; cook until slightly thick. Add molasses and shortening; cool to lukewarm. Soften yeast in warm water in mixing bowl. Add corn mixture; blend well. Add flour gradually to form a stiff dough. Knead about 5 minutes. Place in greased bowl, turning to grease all sides. Cover; let rise in warm place until doubled, about 1 to 1½ hours. Place dough on surface sprinkled with cornmeal. Divide into 2 portions. Shape into 2 loaves. Place in greased pans. Cover; let rise again 1 hour. Bake at 350° for 45 to 55 minutes. YIELD: 2 loaves.

Zucchini Bread

My favorite recipe. Uses half whole-wheat flour!

¾ c. white flour
¾ c. whole-wheat flour
½ c. sugar
1 tsp. baking powder
½ tsp. baking soda
1 tsp. cinnamon
¼ tsp. nutmeg
¼ tsp. cloves
1 egg white
1 egg
¾ c. vegetable oil
1¼ c. unpeeled grated zucchini
1 tsp. vanilla
⅓ c. raisins (optional)

Mix all ingredients in a large bowl. Pour into greased 9 x 5 x 3-inch loaf pan. Bake at 350° for 50 to 60 minutes.

Cornbread

This is a real moist cornbread recipe and good for you!

1¼ c. cornmeal
½ c. sugar
½ tsp. salt
1 c. flour
1 Tbsp. baking powder
1 c. plain yogurt or milk
1 egg
¼ butter or stick margarine, melted

Beat milk, butter, and egg in large bowl. Stir in remaining ingredients all at once just until flour is moistened. Pour into greased 8 x 8-inch pan. Bake 20 to 25 minutes at 400° or until golden brown and a toothpick inserted in center comes out clean.

Irish Soda Bread

2 c. flour
⅓ c. honey
½ tsp salt
1 ½ tsp. baking powder
½ tsp. baking soda
1 Tbsp. melted butter or oil
¾ c. raisins
1 tsp caraway seeds
1 lightly beaten egg
⅔ c. buttermilk or yogurt

Mix first 6 dry ingredients. Mix liquid ingredients. Stir the two together until moistened. Knead a little; shape into a plump disc. Bake in a buttered pan at 350° for 30 to 35 minutes.

Hot Water Gingerbread

This makes a yummy breakfast.

⅓ c. butter
⅔ c. boiling water
1 c. molasses
1¼ c. flour
1 ½ tsp. soda
1 egg
½ tsp. salt
1 tsp. ginger
1 tsp. cinnamon

Melt butter in hot water; add egg, molasses, and dry ingredients. Mix. Bake in shallow 9 x 9-inch pan for 35 to 40 minutes or in greased muffin pans at 350°.

Date and Nut Bread

Great as a breakfast bread or snack!

1 pkg. dates
1 c. sugar
2 ¾ c. bread flour
1 ½ c. boiling water
½ tsp. vanilla
1 Tbsp. melted butter
1 egg
2 tsp. soda
1 c. chopped walnuts

Cut up dates and pour on boiling water. Let stand while preparing the rest. Cream butter and sugar. Add well-beaten egg, flour, soda, and salt. Bake at 350° for 1 hour. Slice thin.

Banana Nut Bread

2 ½ c. all-purpose flour
1 c. sugar
3 ½ tsp. baking soda
1 tsp. salt
3 Tbsp. salad oil
¾ c. milk
1 egg
1 c. mashed ripe bananas
(2 to 3 bananas)
1 c. finely chopped nuts

Heat oven to 350°. Grease and flour 9 x 5 x 3-inch loaf pan or two 8½ x 4½ x 2½-inch loaf pans. Measure all ingredients into large mixer bowl; beat on medium speed ½ minute, scraping side and bottom of bowl constantly. Pour into pan(s). Bake 55 to 65 minutes or until wooden pick inserted in center comes out clean. Remove from pan; cool thoroughly before slicing. YIELD: 1 to 2 loaves.

Pumpkin Bread

This is wonderful for autumn breakfasts and can be made into muffins, too!

⅔ c. shortening
2 ⅔ c. sugar
4 eggs
1 (1 lb) can pumpkin
⅔ c. water
3 ⅓ c. all-purpose flour
2 tsp. baking soda
1 ½ tsp. salt
½ tsp. baking powder
1 tsp. cinnamon
1 tsp. cloves
⅔ c. coarsely chopped nuts
⅔ c. raisins (optional)

Heat oven to 350°. Grease two 9 x 5 x 3-inch loaf pans or three 8½ x 4½ x 2½-inch loaf pans. In large bowl, cream shortening and sugar until fluffy. Stir in eggs, pumpkin, and water. Blend in flour, soda, salt, baking powder, cinnamon and cloves. Stir in nuts and raisins. Pour into pans. Bake about 70 minutes or until wooden pick inserted in center comes out clean.

Welsh Scones

My kids all love these scones. They make a nice breakfast treat.

2 c. flour
½ c. sugar
1 Tbsp. baking powder
½ tsp. salt
2 Tbsp. shortening
¾ c. raisins
1 egg
½ c. milk

In large bowl, mix together all ingredients except raisins. Add raisins; mix. Drop dough by tablespoonsful on greased cookie sheet. Bake at 350° for 20 minutes. YIELD: approximately 12 scones.

Amish Friendship Bread

This is fun to do every once in awhile and share with friends at church!

Starter:

⅔ c. sugar
⅔ c. milk
⅔ c. flour

Combine in large airtight container. Store with the lid on at room temperature. Stir every day for 17 days. ***Do not stir with a metal spoon!***

Day 5 and 10 Add to Starter:

1 c. sugar
1 c. flour
1 c. milk

To Make Bread:

1 c. oil
2 c. flour
1 c. sugar
3 eggs
1 large (6-serving size) box instant vanilla pudding
1 ½ tsp. baking powder
1 tsp. cinnamon
1 tsp. vanilla
½ tsp. soda
½ tsp. salt
1 c. raisins, nuts, coconut, dates, or chocolate chips (optional)

Do not use metal spoon or bowl. Do not refrigerate.
After making the Amish Friendship Bread starter and stirring for 17 days, follow these directions:

Day 1 (18): Already done (leave lid ajar on container).
Days 2, 3, and 4: Stir with wooden spoon.
Day 5: Add preceding ingredients to starter (see above)
Days 6, 7, 8, and 9: Stir.
Day 10: Add to starter (see ingredients above). Stir. Pour off 3 cups into 3 separate containers and share with friends or save one for yourself to begin the 10-day process again. To the remaining starter, add the "make bread" ingredients. Grease 2 loaf pans; sprinkle with a mixture of cinnamon and sugar. Pour batter into pans. Bake 40 to 50 minutes at 350°. Cool 10 minutes. YIELD: 2 loaves.

continued on page 84

Amish Friendship Bread *continued*

Notes:

Starter freezes well. Any flavor instant pudding mix may be substituted for vanilla. You may use plastic Ziploc bags into which to measure starter for friends. And instead of stirring the starter on the days listed, just squeeze the bag. Also, you may use greased and cinnamon-sugared muffin tins or one greased and cinnamon-sugared Bundt cake pan instead of the two loaf pans, if desired.

"Hardee's" Biscuits

I got this recipe from a friend of mine who experimented until she made biscuits that tasted like Hardee's.

5 c. flour
5 tsp. baking powder
1 tsp. baking soda
2 tsp. sugar
1 pkg. yeast
2 c. buttermilk
1 c. Crisco
¼ c. water

Combine flour, baking powder, baking soda, and sugar. Cut in shortening; add buttermilk. Dissolve yeast in water. Combine and mix well. Roll out. Cut into biscuits. Place on ungreased cookie sheet. Bake at 425° for 15 minutes. YIELD: approximately 12–14 biscuits.

Biscuit Mix

A biscuit mix with added nutrition!

1¼ c. unbleached flour
1¼ c. whole-wheat flour
⅛ c. wheat germ
¼ c. soy flour
4 tsp. baking powder
¾ tsp salt
⅔ c. dry milk
scant ½ c. oil

Mix dry ingredients well. Cut in oil with pastry blender. Store in refrigerator. You may use this mix for pancakes, biscuits, plain muffins, or pecan muffins.

Pancakes

1⅓ c. water
1 egg
2 c. Biscuit Mix (see recipe)
1 Tbsp. honey

Combine all ingredients; mix. Cook as you normally cook pancakes. YIELD: 10 pancakes.

Muffins

1 c. water
1 egg
3 c. Biscuit Mix (see recipe)
¼ c. honey

Combine all ingredients; mix. Grease 12 muffin pan cups; fill cups ⅔ full. Bake at 400° for 20 to 25 minutes. YIELD: 1 dozen muffins.

Biscuits

½ c. water
2 c. Biscuit Mix (see recipe)
1 Tbsp honey

Combine all ingredients. Roll dough out to ⅓-inch thickness. Cut into 10 biscuits. Bake at 450° for 10 to 12 minutes. YIELD: 10 biscuits.

Pecan Muffins

6 Tbsp. water
1 egg
2 c. Biscuit Mix (see recipe)
¼ c. honey
½ c. chopped pecans

Combine all ingredients; mix. Grease 8 muffin pan cups; fill cups ⅔ full. Bake at 400° for 20 minutes. YIELD: 8 muffins.

Traditional English Muffins in a Loaf

Very good. A favorite for breakfasts, and it has lots of variations. Can use freshly ground whole wheat flour.

6 c. flour
2 pkg. yeast
1 Tbsp. sugar
2 tsp. salt
¼ tsp. baking soda
2 c. milk
½ c. water
cornmeal

Combine 3 cups of the flour, undissolved yeast, sugar, salt, and soda. Heat milk and water until very warm. Add to dry ingredients. Beat well. Stir in remaining 3 cups of flour to make a stiff batter. Spoon into two 8½ x 4½ x 2½-inch loaf pans, greased and sprinkled with cornmeal. Sprinkle tops with cornmeal. Cover; let rise 45 minutes. Bake at 400° for 25 minutes.

Variations:

Sour Cream and Chives English Muffin Loaf: Add 3 tablespoons freeze-dried chives to dry ingredients before mixing. Add ½ cup milk and ½ cup sour cream with remaining flour. Bake as directed above.

Garlic English Muffin Loaf: Add 2 tablespoons chopped parsley and 1½ teaspoons garlic powder to the dry ingredients before mixing. Proceed as directed above.

Orange Flavored English Muffin Loaf: Add 2 tablespoons grated orange rind to dry ingredients. If desired, substitute orange juice for some of the water. Proceed as directed above.

Pecan Raisin English Muffin Loaf: Add ½ cup chopped pecans and ½ cup raisins to dry ingredients before mixing. Proceed as directed above.

Fruit and Nut English Muffin Loaf: Add 1 cup chopped dates and ½ cup chopped walnuts to dry ingredients before mixing. Proceed as directed above.

Whole Wheat English Muffin Loaf: Use 4 cups white flour and 2 cups whole-wheat flour instead of cups white flour. Add ¼ cup dried currants to dry ingredients before mixing. Proceed as directed above.

Raspberry Cream Cheese Coffeecake

My good friend Lisa makes this for special functions. If you are a raspberry lover, be sure to try this one. It's one of my favorites. In our home one of my daughters began a tradition of fixing a birthday breakfast for each person on their birthday. This is what I always choose!

2 ¼ c. flour
¾ c. sugar
¾ c. butter or margarine
½ tsp. baking powder
½ tsp. baking soda
¼ tsp. salt
¾ c. sour cream
1 tsp. almond extract
1 egg

Filling:

8 oz. cream cheese
¼ c. sugar
1 egg

Topping:

½ c. raspberry jam
½ c. sliced almonds

Heat oven to 350°. Grease and flour 9 or 10-inch springform pan. Combine flour and ¾ cup sugar. Using pastry blender or fork, cut in margarine until mixture resembles coarse crumbs. Reserve 1 cup crumb mixture. To remaining mixture, add baking powder, and salt, sour cream, almond extract, and 1 egg. Blend well. Spread batter over bottom and up sides of pan; should be ¼-inch thick on sides.

In small bowl combine cream cheese, ¼ cup sugar and 1 egg. Blend well. Pour into pan. Carefully spoon preserves over cream cheese mixture.

In small bowl combine reserved crumb mixture and almonds. Sprinkle over preserves.

Bake at 350° for 45 to 55 minutes or until cream cheese is set and crust is golden brown.

Coffee Cake

We don't have this often, but it's a nice treat.

1 ½ c. all-purpose flour
¾ c. sugar
2 ½ tsp. baking powder
¾ tsp. salt
¼ c. shortening
¾ c. milk
topping

Topping:

Mix ⅓ cup packed brown sugar, ¼ cup flour, ½ teaspoon cinnamon, and 3 tablespoons firm butter until crumbly. We often double the topping!

Heat oven to 375°. Grease round layer pan, 9 x 1½-inch or square pan, 8 x 8 x 2-inch, or 9 x 9 x 2-inch. Blend all ingredients except topping; beat vigorously ½ minute. Spread in pan. Sprinkle topping over batter. Bake 25 to 30 minutes or until wooden pick inserted in center comes out clean. Serve warm. YIELD: 9 to 12 servings.

Apple Muffins

1 egg
½ c. milk
¼ c. oil
1 ½ c. flour
½ sugar
1 ½ tsp. cinnamon
2 tsp. baking powder
½ tsp. salt
2 c. chopped apples

Grease muffin tins or put liners in each cup. Preheat oven to 400°. Combine all ingredients; mix well. Bake in preheated oven about 10 to 15 minutes. YIELD: 12 muffins.

Applesauce Bran Muffins

1 ½ c. Nabisco 100% Bran cereal
1 ½ c. applesauce
1 egg
¼ c. melted margarine
½ c. firmly packed brown sugar
1 ½ c. all-purpose flour
1 Tbsp. baking powder
1 tsp. ground cinnamon

Applesauce Glaze (follows)

Mix Bran, applesauce, egg, margarine, and brown sugar; let stand 5 minutes. In large bowl, blend flour, baking powder, and cinnamon; stir in Bran mixture just until blended (batter will be lumpy). Stir in raisins, if desired. Spoon batter into 12 greased 2½-inch muffin pan cups. Bake at 400° for 15 to 18 minutes or until done. Cool slightly. Drizzle with Applesauce Glaze. Serve warm. YIELD: 1 dozen.

Applesauce Glaze:

Blend ½ cup confectioners' sugar into 1 tablespoon applesauce until smooth.

Coconut Raspberry Muffins

- 2 ½ c. all-purpose flour (instead, we use 1 ½ c. whole wheat flour and 1 cup all-purpose)
- 1 Tbsp. baking powder
- 1 c. coconut
- ¾ c. sugar
- 2 eggs, lightly beaten
- 1 c. milk (can substitute ¾ c. coconut milk and ¼ c. milk if you wish)
- 7 Tbsp. butter or margarine, melted
- 4 Tbsp. seedless raspberry jelly or jam

Coconut Crumb Topping:

- ¼ c. all-purpose flour
- ½ c. flaked coconut
- 1 Tbsp. sugar
- 2 Tbsp. butter, cut into small pieces

Preheat oven to 375°. Grease a 12-cup non-stick muffin pan.
For the crumb topping: Place all ingredients in a small bowl and cut in the butter till mixture resembles coarse breadcrumbs.
For the muffins: Mix the flour, baking powder, dried coconut, and sugar in a large bowl. In a separate bowl, mix together eggs, milk, and melted butter. Add the wet ingredients all at once to the dry ingredients and mix briefly. Spoon about half of the batter into greased muffin tins. Make a small hollow in each and fill with 1 tsp. jelly. Top with remaining batter, dividing it evenly. Sprinkle the tops with coconut crumb topping. Bake in oven for 20 minutes or until lightly browned. Cool in pan 10 minutes. Serve warm or cooled. YIELD: 12 muffins.

Lemon Blueberry Muffins

These are real moist and flavorful. This is one of my favorites!

4 eggs
1 c. cooking oil
1 ½ c. sugar
1 tsp. vanilla
rind and juice of 1 lemon
½ c. cornmeal
2 ½ c. flour
2 tsp. baking powder
1 tsp. baking soda
1 c. milk
1 ½ c. blueberries

Beat eggs. Add oil, sugar, vanilla, lemon rind, and juice. Stir in cornmeal. Sift flour, baking powder, and baking soda together. To the batter, add milk, dry ingredients, and blueberries. Stir gently until well mixed. Fill greased muffin cups. Bake at 375° for 20 minutes. YIELD: 18 to 20 muffins.

Zucchini Muffins

A great way to use zucchini from the garden.

2 c. sugar
1 c. vegetable oil
½ c. applesauce
5 egg whites, mixed with fork
1 c. rolled oats
1 ½ c. all-purpose flour
½ c. whole-wheat flour
2 tsp. baking soda
½ tsp. salt
2 tsp. cinnamon
1 large zucchini, shredded

Combine sugar, oil, applesauce, egg whites, and oats. In separate bowl, combine all remaining ingredients except zucchini. Combine sugar/oil mixture with flour mixture. Fold in zucchini. Fill muffin tins and bake at 375° for 25 to 30 minutes, testing for doneness with a toothpick.

Vermont Gingerbread Muffins

If you like gingerbread, you'll love these moist muffins.

½ c. oil
½ c. sugar
½ c. molasses
½ c. sour milk*
2 tsp. baking soda
3 tsp. ground ginger
1 tsp. cinnamon
2 c. flour
2 eggs

*To sour milk, measure 2 teaspoons vinegar into liquid measuring cup. Add milk to make ½ cup.

Grease 12 muffin tins. Combine all ingredients; mix well. Pour into greased muffin tins (or liners, if you like). Bake at 325° for 20 to 25 minutes. YIELD: 12 muffins.

Refrigerator Bran Muffins

This is our favorite bran muffin recipe. They're full of fiber and great for you. The batter keeps for several weeks in the refrigerator although ours never stays there that long! Rick will often cook a couple fresh in the microwave muffin pans before work in the morning.

2 c. ready-to-eat bran cereal
(Nabisco "100% Bran" cereal is best)
2 c. boiling water
1 c. shortening or margarine
1 ½ c. sugar
4 additional cups bran cereal
4 eggs
1 qt. buttermilk
5 c. flour
5 tsp. soda
1 tsp. salt

Measure 2 cups bran cereal into a bowl. Pour boiling water over it; set aside to cool.

In a large mixing bowl, cream together shortening or margarine, sugar, and eggs. Add buttermilk and soaked bran mixture; beat in. Sift together flour, soda, and salt; add dry ingredients to creamed mixture and fold until flour is moistened. Fold in additional 4 cups bran cereal. Store batter in covered containers in refrigerator. Keeps 3 to 4 weeks.

When ready to bake, preheat oven to 400° and fill well-greased muffin tins ⅔ full. Bake 20 minutes.

Optional: Raisins or nuts may be added just before baking.

Chocolate Chip Muffins

These have relatively little sugar, considering their name. My family loves them. They round out a meal of pasta real well.

2 c. white flour
1 Tbsp. baking powder
½ tsp salt
½ c. sugar
1 egg, slightly beaten
1 c. milk
¼ c. melted butter
1 c. semi-sweet chocolate chips

Preheat oven to 375°. Grease muffin pans. Mix the flour, baking powder, salt, and sugar in a large bowl. Add the egg, milk, and butter, stirring only enough to dampen the flour; the batter should not be smooth. Fold in chocolate chips. Spoon into the muffin pans, filling each cup about ⅔ full. Bake 20 to 25 minutes. YIELD: 12 muffins.

Peanut Butter Chocolate Chip Muffins or Bread

These are a breakfast favorite. Good for you.

1 ½ c. whole wheat flour
1 ½ c. ground oats
1 ½ tsp. baking powder
1 tsp. soda
1 tsp. salt
1 c. peanut butter
½ c. butter or margarine
¼ c. sugar
¼ c. brown sugar
2 eggs
1 ½ c. sour milk*
2 tsp. vanilla
approximately 1 c. chocolate chips

*Note: To make milk sour for baking add 1 Tbsp. vinegar for each cup of milk used.

Mix together peanut butter, butter, and sugars until smooth. Beat in eggs. Add sour milk and vanilla and beat until smooth. Add flour, ground oats, baking powder, soda, and salt. Mix in chocolate chips with a spoon. Bake loaves at 350° for 40 to 45 minutes, or muffins at 375° for 13 to 15 minutes Makes two loaves of bread or 24 muffins.

Sweet New England Blueberry Muffins

These are sweet, but a real treat! A New England favorite.

½ c. margarine
¾ c. granulated sugar
2 eggs
2 tsp. baking powder
2 c. flour
pinch of salt
½ c. milk
¾ c. blueberries
cinnamon and sugar

Cream margarine and sugar. Add eggs, flour, baking powder, salt, and milk; mix thoroughly. Fold in blueberries; don't stir more than a few seconds or the batter will turn purple! Grease muffin tins. Fill ¾ full. Sprinkle cinnamon and sugar on top of each. Bake at 375° for 20 minutes. YIELD: 20 muffins.

Mom's Cream Puffs

This was a special treat when we were kids. If Mom knew we'd had a bad day at school, she'd bake them for dessert that night to cheer us up.

¼ c. butter
½ c. boiling water
½ c. bread flour
2 unbeaten eggs

Add butter to water; heat until butter melts. Add flour all at once and stir vigorously until ball farms in center of pan. Remove from heat; add eggs, one at a time, beating after adding each egg. Mixture should be very stiff. Makes 6 large puffs or 18 tiny ones. Shape on buttered cookie sheet, dropping from spoon. Bake until free of beads of moisture at 375°. If in doubt, remove one from oven to test. Fill with Cream Filling.

Cream Filling:

⅔ c. sugar
⅓ c. bread flour
⅛ tsp. salt
2 c. scalded milk
1 tsp. vanilla or ½ tsp. lemon extract
2 eggs

continued on page 94

Mom's Cream Puffs *continued*

Mix dry ingredients. Add scalded milk gradually. Cook 15 minutes in a double boiler, stirring constantly until mixture thickens and afterward stir occasionally. Add eggs, slightly beaten, and cook 3 minutes. Cool and flavor. For thicker filling, use ½ cup flour.

Cream Puff Filling

1 egg
3 Tbsp. flour
⅓ c. sugar
pinch of salt
1 c. milk
1 tsp. vanilla

In saucepan, mix egg, sugar, flour, salt, and milk. Cook over low heat, stirring occasionally, Beat occasionally with spoon until smooth and thick. Add vanilla and cool. When cold, fill cream puffs and frost as desired with confectioners' sugar frosting glaze.

No-Roll Pie Crust

If you're in a hurry, this is a great pie crust you can make quickly; it's very good, too.

1 ½ c. flour
½ c. oil
2 Tbsp. milk
1 tsp. sugar
pinch of salt

Measure flour directly into pie plate. Measure oil into measuring cup; mix milk into oil. Pour into pie plate. Add salt and sugar; mix all ingredients well with a fork. Press against the sides of the pie plate. YIELD: 1 pie crust.

Double Layer Pumpkin Pie

4 oz. cream cheese, softened
1 Tbsp. milk or half and half
1 Tbsp. sugar
1 ½ c. whipped topping
1 graham cracker crust
1 c. cold milk or half and half
1 (16 oz.) can pumpkin
2 (4-serving size) pkg. instant vanilla pudding
1 tsp. ground cinnamon
½ tsp. ground ginger
¼ tsp. ground cloves

Mix cream cheese, 1 tablespoon milk, and sugar in large bowl with wire whisk until smooth. Gently stir in whipped topping. Spread on bottom of crust.

Pour 1 cup cold milk into bowl. Add pumpkin, pudding mixes, and spices. Beat with wire whisk until well mixed. (Mixture will be thick.) Spread over cream cheese layer. Refrigerate 4 hours or until set. Garnish with additional whipped topping, if desired. Store leftover pie in refrigerator. YIELD: 8 servings.

Variation: Stir ¼ cup toasted chopped pecans into cream cheese mixture. Spread on bottom of crust. Continue as directed above.

No-Bake Pumpkin Pie

1 envelope unflavored gelatin
1 tsp. ground cinnamon
½ tsp. ground ginger
½ tsp. ground nutmeg
½ tsp. salt
1 (14 oz.) can sweetened condensed milk
2 eggs, well beaten
1 (16 oz.) can pumpkin (about 2 c.)
1 graham cracker crust

In heavy medium-sized saucepan, combine gelatin, cinnamon, ginger, nutmeg, and salt; stir in milk and eggs. Mix well. Let stand 1 minute. Over low heat, cook and stir constantly until gelatin dissolves and thickens slightly (about 10 minutes). Remove from heat. Stir in pumpkin; mix well. Pour into crust. Chill 3 hours or until set. YIELD: 1 pie.

Toll House Pie

2 eggs
½ c. flour
½ c. sugar
½ c. light brown sugar
¾ c. softened butter or margarine
1 c. chopped walnuts or pecans
1 (6 oz.) pkg. semi-sweet chocolate chips
1 prepared 8 or 9-inch pie shell

Beat eggs until foamy at high speed, 3 minutes. Beat in flour, sugars, then margarine. Stir in nuts and chocolate chips. Pour into pie shell. Bake at 325° for 55 to 60 minutes. Serve hot with ice cream or whipped cream, if desired. YIELD: 1 pie (6 to 8 servings).

Chocolate Chess Pie

This is a very rich pie, so we generally only have it on very special occasions, like on Thanksgiving and Christmas.

1 stick butter
¼ c. milk
1 Tbsp. flour or cornmeal
1 tsp. vanilla
2 sq. unsweetened chocolate
2 eggs, beaten
1¼ c. sugar

Melt butter and chocolate. Add sugar, then eggs, milk, flour, and vanilla. Mix well and pour into unbaked pie shell. Bake at 325° for 40 minutes.

Strawberry Pie

1 baked 9-inch pie crust
2 pt. strawberries
whipped cream
1 c. sugar
1 c. boiling water
2 ½ Tbsp. cornstarch
2 Tbsp. strawberry-flavored gelatin

Mix sugar and cornstarch; stir into water. Boil until thick and clear. Add gelatin; stir until dissolved. Cool. Clean and stem strawberries. Arrange in crust. Pour glaze over strawberries. Chill and top with whipped cream. YIELD: 1 pie.

Fresh Rhubarb Pie

1 (8-inch) two crust pie pastry
4 c. fresh rhubarb, cut in ½-inch pieces
1 to 1¼ c. sugar
¼ c. flour
¼ tsp. grated orange peel (if desired)
1 Tbsp. butter or margarine

Heat oven to 425°. Stir together flour, sugar, and orange peel. Turn half the rhubarb into pastry lined pie pan; sprinkle with half the sugar mixture. Repeat with remaining rhubarb and sugar. Dot with butter. Cover with top crust which has slits cut in it; seal and flute. Sprinkle with sugar. Cover edge with 2 to 3-inch strip of aluminum foil to prevent excessive browning; remove foil last 15 minutes of baking. Bake 40 to 50 minutes or until crust is brown and juice begins to bubble through slits in crust.

Strawberry Rhubarb Crumb Pie

When I was a girl, my parents always grew rhubarb in their garden. They gave me a start from their plants, and I've grown it ever since.

1 egg
1 c. sugar
2 Tbsp. all-purpose flour
1 tsp. vanilla extract
¾ lb. fresh rhubarb, cut into ½-inch pieces (about 3 c.)
1 pt. fresh strawberries, halved
1 unbaked pie shell (9-inch)

Topping:

¾ c. all-purpose flour
½ c. packed brown sugar
½ c. butter or margarine
½ c. quick-cooking or rolled oats

In a mixing bowl, beat egg. Beat in sugar, flour, and vanilla; mix well. Gently fold in rhubarb and strawberries. Pour into pie shell.

For topping, combine flour, brown sugar, and oats in a small bowl; cut in butter until crumbly. Sprinkle over fruit. Bake at 400° for 10 minutes. Reduce heat to 350°. Bake for 35 minutes or until golden brown and bubbly. YIELD: 8 servings.

Turtle Cheesecake p. 128

Hot Fudge Ice Cream Cake p. 130

Peanut Butter Chocolate Chip Cookies p. 113

Cakes, Cookies & Desserts

Cakes, Cookies & Desserts

Mississippi Mud Cake

When one of my sons was little, we baked this cake for Rick a day or two before Father's Day. When Daddy came home from work that evening, my then 3-year-old son ran to the door, excited about the surprise, and said, "Daddy, Daddy, we made you a Methsy-thethsy Mud Cake!"

2 c. sugar
4 eggs, beaten
1 c. margarine or butter
½ c. cocoa
1 ½ c. flour
dash of salt
1 tsp. vanilla
1 ½ c. chopped pecans
1 small pkg. miniature marshmallows

Melt butter and cocoa together in saucepan. Remove from heat and stir in sugar. Add a little of the hot mixture to the eggs to prevent curdling. Add remainder of eggs and mix well. Add flour, salt, and vanilla. Bake in 9 x 13-inch baking pan for 35 to 40 minutes at 350°. Sprinkle nuts and marshmallows on top of hot cake and return to oven for about 3 minutes until marshmallows puff up. Frost with the following:

Frosting:

1 stick soft margarine
½ c. milk
1 box powdered sugar
⅓ c. cocoa
Mix over low heat until smooth enough to cover the nuts and marshmallows.

Quick-Mix Chocolate Cake

All this mixes up in one pan; quick, easy, and good!

1 ½ c. flour
⅓ c. cocoa
1 tsp. salt
1 tsp. soda
1 c. sugar
1 c. water
1 Tbsp. vinegar
⅓ c. oil
1 ½ tsp. vanilla

Combine all ingredients in a 9 x 9-inch baking pan; stir with a fork. Bake at 375° for 30 minutes. Frost, if desired.

Punch Bowl Cake

My son Rick was born on my birthday. This is his choice of birthday cake each year.

1 yellow cake mix baked into 2 round layers
1 large (16-20 oz.) can cherry pie filling
2 (6 oz.) pkg. frozen coconut
1 large (32 oz.) can fruit cocktail, drained
1 ½ c. chopped nuts
1 (20 oz.) can crushed pineapple, drained
2 (8 oz.) containers Cool Whip
1 large or 2 small pkg. instant vanilla pudding

Bake layer cake according to package directions; cool completely. Prepare instant pudding as directed on box. Refrigerate until set. Place a cake layer on the bottom of a 6-quart punch bowl or other large bowl. Add, in layers, half of all ingredients in this order: pudding, pie filling, fruit cocktail, crushed pineapple, nuts, coconut, and 1 container Cool Whip. Add second layer and add other half in same order. Garnish with coconut, nuts, and cherries or strawberries. If desired, strawberry pie filling may be substituted for cherry. Refrigerate cake overnight. YIELD: 20 to 30 servings.

Mini Chip Pound Cake

This is one of the kids' favorite things to bake; even my boys liked making it when they were younger. We make it sometimes for company.

1 c. butter
2 c. sugar
1 ½ tsp. vanilla
3 eggs
3 c. unsifted flour
2 tsp. baking powder
½ tsp. salt
1 c. milk
1 ½ c. mini chocolate chips*

*Milk chocolate or semi-sweet. Regular size chips may be substituted, if desired.

Combine butter, sugar, and vanilla; cream until light and fluffy. Add eggs; beat well. Combine flour, baking powder, and salt. Add alternately with milk to creamed mixture, beating until smooth. Stir in chips. Pour into greased and floured 10-inch tube pan or Bundt pan. Bake at 350° for 1 hour or until done. Cool completely. Remove from pan and glaze.

Glaze:

2 Tbsp. sugar
2 Tbsp. water
½ c. chips
1 Tbsp. Marshmallow Creme or 2 to 3 marshmallows

Bring sugar and water to a boil in small saucepan; remove from heat. Immediately add chips. Stir until melted. Blend in Marshmallow Creme or marshmallows. Add hot water, ½ teaspoon at a time, until desired consistency.

Collector's Cocoa Cake

I got the recipe for this cake from a can of cocoa many years ago and it's been a favorite of ours ever since.

¾ c. shortening, margarine, or butter
1¾ c. sugar
2 eggs
1 tsp. vanilla
¾ c. cocoa
1¼ tsp. baking soda
½ tsp. salt
1⅓ c. water
2 c. flour

Cream butter and sugar. Add eggs. Mix dry ingredients together and add alternately with water using electric mixer. Beat well. Pour into greased and floured pan(s); you may use one 9 x 13-inch baking pan or 2 layer cake pans, 8 or 9-inch. Bake 35 to 40 minutes at 350° or until cake tests done. Cool completely before icing. YIELD: 12 to 14 servings.

Daffodil Angel Cake

My mom used to bake this cake for all our birthdays when we were growing up. Even after Mom died several years ago, my sister continued to bake it for my dad each year on his birthday.

White Part:

6 egg whites
½ tsp. cream of tartar
⅛ tsp. salt
¾ c. sugar
½ c. flour
½ tsp. vanilla

Beat egg whites with electric mixer on high speed until foamy. Add cream of tartar and salt; beat until stiff. Sift sugar and flour together four times and fold into egg whites with low speed of electric mixer. Add vanilla.

Yellow Part:

6 egg yolks
¾ c. sugar
⅛ tsp. salt
¾ c. flour
1 tsp. baking powder
¼ c. boiling water
½ tsp. lemon extract

Beat egg yolks, sugar, and salt together on high speed of electric mixer for 3 minutes or until very light and thick. Sift flour and baking powder together four times and add to egg mixture with mixer on low speed. Increase speed and slowly add boiling water and lemon extract. Pour into large ungreased angel cake pan, alternating yellow and white mixtures. Bake 1 hour and 15 minutes in 325° oven. Invert cake on cooler. Allow to cool before removing from pan.

Winter Squash Cake with Penuche Icing

½ c. butter
1 ½ c. sugar
2 eggs
¾ c. squash puree
1 ½ tsp. vanilla
2 ¼ c. flour
2 tsp. baking powder
1 tsp. baking soda
½ tsp. allspice
½ tsp. cinnamon
¼ tsp. nutmeg
¼ tsp. cloves
½ c. sour milk

Preheat oven to 350°. Cream butter and sugar; add eggs. Stir in puree and vanilla. Add dry ingredients alternately with sour milk. Bake 45 minutes. See following recipe for Penuche Icing.

Penuche Icing

2 c. brown sugar
⅓ c. water
1 egg white
⅛ tsp. salt
1 tsp. vanilla
12 pecan halves

Dissolve sugar in water; stir once. Continue to boil without stirring until syrup reaches soft-ball stage (234°). Beat whites with salt until frothy. Add hot syrup in thin stream, beating constantly. Continue beating until thick enough to hold shape. Stir in vanilla. Frost cooled cake; garnish with pecan halves.

Carrot Cake

During each Christmas season, we used to bake this cake for a birthday cake for Jesus. We would frost it with Cream Cheese Frosting (recipe follows) and the kids would write "Happy Birthday, Jesus" on the cake with raisins.

2 c. sugar
1 ½ c. vegetable oil
4 eggs
3 ½ c. grated carrots (about 6 carrots)
2 c. sifted flour
1 Tbsp. cinnamon
1 ½ tsp. allspice
1 tsp. cloves
½ c. pecans, chopped

Blend sugar, oil, and eggs. Add dry ingredients to the first mixture and blend. Now add carrots and then blend in nuts. Bake in preheated 300° oven until done, about 40 to 60 minutes, using an ungreased 9 x 13-inch pan. Cool cake and top with Cream Cheese frosting (recipe follows).

Cream Cheese Frosting:

1 lb. powdered sugar
8 oz. softened cream cheese
2 tsp. vanilla
½ c. butter or margarine, softened

Blend in mixture and spread on cooled carrot cake.

Chocolate Raspberry Cake

My daughter Carrie made this for me for Mother's Day this year. I LOVE raspberry and chocolate and this is so delicious.

1 ½ c sugar
1 c. canola oil
1 c. milk
1 c. warm water
2 Tbsp. instant coffee granules
(more or less to suit tastes)
2 eggs
1 ½ tsp. vanilla extract
2 c. all-purpose flour
¾ c. baking cocoa
2 tsp. baking soda
1 tsp. baking powder
1 tsp. salt

In a large bowl, beat wet ingredients until well mixed. Add dry ingredients and beat until thoroughly combined. Pour into two 9-inch round cake pans. Bake at 325° for approximately 35 minutes. Allow to cool.

Chocolate Raspbery Ganache:

⅔ c. heavy cream
2 c. semi-sweet chocolate chips
½ c. red raspberry preserves
4 Tbsp. butter

In a small, heavy saucepan over medium heat, bring the heavy cream to a simmer; remove pan from heat. Add the chocolate chips, preserves, and butter, and stir until melted. Cool completely and whip to desired spreading consistency using an electric mixer on medium speed.

When cakes are cool, take out of pans. Spread half the ganache on bottom layer. Top with second cake layer. To remaining ganache add enough confectioner's sugar and milk to reach desired consistency for icing. YIELD: 12-16 servings

Peanut Butter Cake

One of our very favorite cakes! This recipe is from Rick's mom.

½ c. softened butter or margarine
1 ½ c. sugar
2¼ c. sifted flour
1 Tbsp. baking powder
1 tsp. salt
⅓ c. peanut butter
1 c. milk
2 eggs
1 tsp. vanilla

Cream butter. Sift in sugar, flour, baking powder, and salt. Add peanut butter and ⅔ cup milk. Beat 2 minutes on low speed with electric mixer, or 300 strokes by hand. Add remaining ⅓ cup milk, vanilla, and eggs. Beat 2 minutes. Pour into 9 x 13-inch greased baking pan or two 9-inch greased layer cake pans. Bake at 375° for 25 minutes. Frost with Chocolate Peanut Butter Frosting.

Chocolate Peanut Butter Frosting:

⅓ c. cocoa
½ c. peanut butter
2 ⅔ c. powdered sugar
¼ tsp. salt
½ c. cream or evaporated milk
1 tsp. vanilla

Cream cocoa and peanut butter. Add remaining ingredients. Beat until smooth; spread on cooled cake.

Chocolate Peanut Butter Cupcakes

Delicious, with a surprise in the middle.

1 c. flour
⅓ c. cocoa
¾ tsp. baking soda
½ tsp. salt
⅓ c. margarine or shortening
1 c. packed brown sugar
2 eggs
½ c. milk

Mix like a cake. Grease muffin tins or use cupcake liners; put 2 tablespoons of batter into each cup or liner. Add 1 teaspoon filling, then more batter. Do not stir filling into batter. Bake at 375° for 20 minutes and frost as desired.

Filling:

3 oz. cream cheese
¼ c. peanut butter
1 Tbsp. honey
1 Tbsp. milk

Mix together until well blended.

Orange Pineapple Cake

1 yellow boxed cake mix
1 (15 oz.) can mandarin oranges, undrained
4 eggs
½ c. oil

Mix well. Pour into two greased and floured layer pans. Bake at 350° until done, approximately 20 minutes. Cool.

Icing:

1 large carton Cool Whip
1 (5 ½ oz.) box vanilla pudding
1 (15 ½ oz.) can crushed pineapple

Drain pineapple. Combine ingredients and mix for 5 minutes. Ice cooled cake. Store in refrigerator.

Mom's Vanilla Frosting

2 to 2 ½ Tbsp. shortening
2 c. confectioners' sugar
pinch of salt
milk (to make right consistency)
1 tsp. vanilla
2 Tbsp. Marshmallow Creme

Combine all ingredients except milk; stir and blend. Slowly add milk to make right consistency. Spread over cooled cake.

Caramel Frosting

¼ c. margarine
½ c. packed brown sugar
1¼ c. sifted powdered sugar
¼ tsp. vanilla
2 Tbsp. milk

Melt margarine. Stir in brown sugar. Cook 2 minutes over low heat while stirring constantly until it comes to a boil. Remove from heat and gradually stir in confectioners' sugar, vanilla, and milk; stir well. Frosts a 9 x 13-inch sheet cake. (To frost a layer cake, you'll need to double the recipe.)

Best-Ever Chocolate Frosting

4 Tbsp. milk
4 Tbsp. cocoa
1 stick margarine
1 tsp. vanilla
1 box (approximately 4 c.) sifted confectioners' sugar

Boil first 3 ingredients 1½ minutes, stirring constantly over medium heat; cool slightly. Add vanilla and sugar. Keep warm. Pour over hot sheet cake.

Decorators' Icing

2 lb. sifted confectioners' sugar
1 c. shortening (vegetable Crisco)
¼ tsp. salt
½ scant c. water
2 tsp. colorless vanilla

Cream sugar and shortening; add remaining ingredients and mix well on low speed.

Mom's Chocolate Frosting

½ c. butter or margarine
2 c. confectioners' sugar
pinch of salt
1 tsp. vanilla
2 sq. unsweetened chocolate or ⅓ c. cocoa
¼ c. milk

Combine sugar, salt, and vanilla in bowl. Melt shortening with chocolate in saucepan. When melted, add to sugar mixture in bowl. Heat milk and add slowly. Beat vigorously until right consistency.

Variation (Chocolate Peanut Butter Frosting):

equal amounts brown sugar and confectioners' sugar
2 Tbsp peanut butter
1 to 2 Tbsp. cream or butter

Prepare as directed above.

French Silk Frosting

2 ⅔ c. confectioners' sugar
⅔ c. soft butter
2 Tbsp. milk
2 oz. unsweetened melted chocolate, cooled
¾ tsp. vanilla

In small mixer bowl, blend sugar, butter, chocolate, and vanilla on low speed. Gradually add milk; beat until smooth and fluffy. YIELD: enough frosting for two 9-inch layers or three 8-inch layers.

Chocolate Chipper Champs

¾ c. margarine
1⅓ c. brown sugar
2 eggs
1 tsp. vanilla
2¼ c. flour
1 tsp. soda
½ tsp. salt
1 c. M&M's
½ c. chopped nuts

Beat together margarine and sugar; blend in eggs and vanilla. Add remaining ingredients. Mix well. Grease cookie sheets; drop dough by tablespoonsful 3 inches apart on sheets. Press 3 to 4 additional candies into each. Bake at 350° for 10 to 12 minutes. YIELD: 2 dozen 3½-inch cookies.

Chewy Jumbo Chocolate Chip Cookies

I think my daughter Kate found this recipe initially, but Kelley makes these for a special treat in our home.

4¼ cups all –purpose flour
1 tsp. baking powder
1 tsp. soda
1 tsp. salt
1 ½ c. butter, softened
1 ¼ c. firmly packed brown sugar
2 eggs
1 Tbsp. vanilla
1 (12 oz.) pkg. chocolate chips

Heat oven to 375°. Combine butter, sugar, and brown sugar in a large bowl. Beat at medium speed, scraping bowl often till creamy. Add eggs and vanilla. Continue beating until well mixed. Gradually add flour, baking powder, salt, and soda. Beat at low speed till well mixed. Stir in chocolate chips. Drop dough by ¼ cupfuls, 2 inches apart, onto ungreased cookie sheets. Bake 10–14 minutes or until light golden brown. Cool 1 minute, remove to cooling racks. YIELD: 26 jumbo cookies.

Ritz Cookies

This recipe is from Rick's mom, Grannie.

Ritz crackers
peanut butter
melted semi-sweet chocolate chips or chocolate almond bark

Spread peanut butter on a cracker; top with another cracker. Dip in melted chocolate; let dry on waxed paper. Store in refrigerator.
Variation: Follow directions above except melt 4 blocks white almond bark and 1 c. chocolate chips together. Add ½ tsp. mint flavoring. Dip crackers with tongs and place on sheets of waxed paper. Store in refrigerator.

Pecan Dainties

When I was growing up, my Auntie Dot would bake these cookies for every family get-together/special occasion.

½ c. butter or margarine
2 Tbsp. granulated sugar
1 tsp. vanilla
1 c. all-purpose flour
1 c. chopped pecans
powdered sugar

Thoroughly mix softened butter, sugar, and vanilla by hand. Gradually stir in flour and pecans. Chill. Shape into small balls. Bake on ungreased baking sheets for 15 to 17 minutes until firm but not brown. Roll gently in powdered sugar. Cool; sugar again. YIELD: 50 cookies.

Grandma's Sturbridge Hobnails

This is an old New England cookie recipe, probably receiving its name from Sturbridge Village near where Grandma lived in Massachusetts. Shortly after I got married, I asked her to send me her favorite cookie recipe and this is the one she sent.

½ c. butter or margarine
1 c. brown sugar
1 beaten egg
1 tsp. vanilla
1 ½ c. flour
½ tsp. baking powder
½ tsp. soda
¼ tsp. salt
½ c. raisins
½ c. chocolate chips

Cream butter and brown sugar. Add egg and vanilla. Stir in flour, soda, baking powder, and salt. Add raisins and chocolate chips. Drop in greased cookie sheet 2 inches apart. Bake at 375° for 8 minutes or until golden brown. YIELD: 3½ dozen.

Peanut Butter Oatmeal Chocolate Chip Cookies

This is a recipe my aunt sent to my daughter Kate.

2 sticks margarine
1 c. sugar
1 c. light brown sugar
1 c. peanut butter
3 eggs
1 tsp. vanilla
1 ⅔ c. flour
1 tsp. baking soda
2 c. Quick Quaker oats
6 oz. chocolate chips

continued on page 110

Peanut Butter Oatmeal Chocolate Chip Cookies *continued*

Cream margarine and sugars. Add peanut butter and cream well. Add eggs and vanilla. Combine flour and soda; add to creamed ingredients. Add oatmeal; mix well. Add chocolate chips and stir with wooden spoon. Drop by spoonfuls onto cookie sheets. Bake at 350° for 15 minutes.

Brown Edge Cookies

I remember making these cookies with my mother and sisters when I was little. Our job was to stamp the cookies with the cloth-covered glass. Sometimes Mom would decorate them with a cherry or colored jimmies on each cookie.

1 c. shortening
½ tsp. salt
⅔ c. sugar
2 eggs
1 tsp. vanilla or grated orange rind
2 c. flour

Combine shortening, salt, and vanilla. Add sugar gradually. Add beaten eggs; add flour and mix well. Drop by teaspoonsful on greased baking sheet. Cover the bottom of a glass with a cloth dampened in cold water (wring well). Stamp each cookie with cloth-covered glass. Bake at 350° until done.

Famous Oatmeal Cookies

¾ c. shortening
1 c. brown sugar
½ c. granulated sugar
1 egg
1 tsp. salt
1 tsp. vanilla
½ tsp. soda
¼ c. water
1 c. flour
3 c. oats
1 to 2 c. chocolate chips
raisins (if desired)
coconut (optional)
candy (optional)

Cream shortening with water, sugars, and egg. Add soda, salt, and vanilla. Stir in oats and flour. Add chips, raisins, coconut, or candy as desired. Drop by teaspoonsful onto ungreased cookie sheets. Bake at 350° for 10 to 12 minutes. YIELD: approximately 6 dozen.

No-Bake Chocolate Oatmeal Cookies

I got this recipe from my cousin way back when I was in seventh grade. Once when I was spending the day at her house, we made these and I got the recipe from her then. If you find you need a dessert and fast. these are very quick to make.

½ c. cocoa
½ c. (1 stick) butter or margarine
½ c. milk
2 c. sugar
3 to 4 c. oats
1 tsp. vanilla

Combine cocoa, milk, margarine, and sugar; boil for 3 minutes. Add oats and vanilla; mix well. Drop by spoonfuls onto ungreased cookie sheets. Store in refrigerator.

Peanut Butter Blossoms

(Yummy!)

½ c. shortening
¾ c. creamy peanut butter
⅓ c. granulated sugar
⅓ c. light brown sugar
1 egg
2 Tbsp. milk
1 tsp. vanilla
1 ½ c. flour
1 tsp. baking soda
½ tsp. salt
additional granulated sugar
1 (10 oz.) pkg. Hershey's Kisses

Heat oven to 375°. In a large mixer bowl, beat shortening and peanut butter until well blended. Add ⅓ cup granulated sugar and the brown sugar; beat well until light and fluffy. Add egg, milk, and vanilla; beat well. Stir together flour, soda, and salt; gradually add to peanut butter mixture. Shape dough into 1-inch balls. Roll in granulated sugar; place on ungreased cookie sheet. Bake 8 to 10 minutes, or until lightly browned. Immediately place 1 Kiss (unless you're using mini Kisses, in which case use 3 Kisses) on top of each cookie, pressing down slightly. Remove from cookie sheet to wire cooling rack. Cool completely. YIELD: about 4 dozen.

Monster Cookies

6 eggs
2¼ c. brown sugar
1 c. margarine
2 c. white sugar
4 tsp. baking soda
½ tsp. Karo syrup (optional)
1 ½ tsp. vanilla
3 c. crunchy peanut butter
7 c. rolled oats
2 c. flour
8 oz. chocolate chips
½ lb. M&M's

Mix eggs, sugars, margarine, soda, corn syrup, vanilla, and peanut butter with mixer. Stir in remaining ingredients. Drop by ¼ cupfuls onto greased baking sheets. Bake at 350° for 10 minutes.

Peanut Butter Bars

⅓ c. margarine
½ c. peanut butter
¾ c. sugar
1 tsp. vanilla
2 eggs
1 c. flour
1 tsp. baking powder
1 c. semi-sweet chocolate chips

Preheat oven to 350°. Grease a 9 x 13-inch pan. Combine all ingredients except chocolate chips; mix thoroughly and spread in prepared pan. Sprinkle chocolate chips on top. Place in oven for 3 minutes and marbelize the chips. Return to oven and bake for 30 minutes.

Kris' Chocolate Chip Cookies

This is our favorite chocolate chip cookie recipe. Sometimes we bake it in a round cookie sheet or pizza pan and decorate with icing when cool for a special gift for a birthday or other special occasion.

2¼ c. flour
1 tsp. baking soda
1 tsp. salt
1 c. shortening
¾ c. sugar
¾ c. brown sugar
1 tsp. vanilla
½ tsp. water
2 eggs
½ pkg. chocolate chips
¼ c. chopped nuts

Sift together flour, baking soda, and salt. In a separate bowl, combine shortening and sugars; cream. Add vanilla and water. Beat until creamy. Beat in eggs. Add dry mixture. Stir in chocolate chips and nuts. Drop by teaspoonsful onto greased cookie sheets. Bake at 375° for 10 to 12 minutes. Or spread dough in greased 15 x 10-inch pan. Bake at 375° for 20 minutes. Cut into bars.

Variation: For Double Chocolate Chip Cookies, add ⅓ cup cocoa to dry ingredients and 1 teaspoon water to creamed mixture. Proceed as directed above. (This works with any chocolate chip cookie recipe.)

Peanut Butter Chocolate Chip Cookies

(See photo on page 99.)

½ c. margarine
½ c. sugar
½ c. brown sugar
¾ c. peanut butter
1 egg
½ tsp. vanilla
1¼ c. flour
½ tsp. baking soda
½ tsp. baking powder
¼ tsp. salt
2 c. chocolate chips

Cream together the margarine, sugar, brown sugar, and peanut butter. Add egg and vanilla. Mix well. Stir in flour, baking soda, baking powder, salt, and chocolate chips. Mix thoroughly. Spoon onto cookie sheets. Bake in 350° oven for 8 to 10 minutes or until done.

Variation: M&M's can be substituted for chocolate chips.

Mom's Peanut Butter Cookies

This was my mom's special recipe. I remember helping her do the crisscrossing with a fork when I was very small.

1 c. shortening
1 c. peanut butter
1 c. granulated sugar
1 c. brown sugar
1 tsp. vanilla
2 unbeaten eggs
1 ½ c. flour
1 tsp. baking soda
½ tsp. salt

Cream shortening, peanut butter, and sugars; add eggs, vanilla, and salt and mix well. Stir in remaining ingredients. Roll into balls; dip in sugar and crisscross with a fork. Bake at 325° for 15 to 20 minutes. YIELD: 6 dozen.

Lever House Macaroons

Mom made these cookies frequently, but when we had parties at school she would make them larger and insert straws in them so we could hold them like a lollipop. They were a favorite with all the kids. Sometimes she'd put candy corns on them for eyes, nose, and mouth. The cookies have a really good taste.

How fun to pass on this tradition with my granddaughter Anne.

1 c. shortening
¾ c. firmly packed brown sugar
¾ c. granulated sugar
½ tsp. salt
½ tsp. vanilla
½ tsp. cinnamon
2 unbeaten eggs
½ c. chopped walnuts
1¼ c. flour
1 tsp. soda
3 c. rolled oats

Combine shortening, sugars, vanilla, salt, cinnamon, and eggs. Beat thoroughly. Stir in walnuts. Sift together flour and soda. Add to shortening mixture and blend. Stir in oats. Place dough by tablespoonsful on greased cookie sheets, leaving a little space between. Press with a fork. Bake in 350° oven for 12 to 14 minutes. Cool about 2 minutes before removing from sheet. YIELD: 5½ dozen.

Variation: For Lollipop Cookies, prepare dough as directed above. Just before baking, insert a lollipop stick, paper drinking straw, or wooden skewer into each mound of dough with sticks parallel to the sheet to make it look like a lollipop. Decorate with facial features (use M&M's, gumdrops, raisins, candy corns, etc.). Bake as directed.

Peanutty Chewy Bars

This recipe was made for us by my daughter-in-law. It fast became a favorite!

1¼ c. unsifted flour
⅔ c. granulated sugar
¼ c. firmly packed light brown sugar
1 tsp. baking powder
¼ tsp. salt
½ c. cold butter
2 eggs, beaten
1 (10 oz.) pkg. peanut butter chips
1 (14 oz.) can sweetened condensed milk
1 c. flaked coconut

Preheat oven to 350°. Stir together flour, sugars, cocoa, baking powder, and salt. Cut in butter until crumbly. Add eggs; mix well. Spread in greased 9 x 13-inch baking pan. Bake 8 minutes. Remove from oven; top evenly with chips, then condensed milk and coconut. Return to oven; bake 20 minutes or until lightly browned. Cool. Garnish with Drizzle. Cut into bars.

Drizzle:

Melt ½ cup semi-sweet chips with 1½ teaspoons shortening. Stir until smooth. YIELD: 24 to 36 bars.

Seven Layer Cookies

An easy recipe from my mom.

½ stick margarine
1 ½ c. graham cracker crumbs
1 c. semi-sweet chocolate chips
½ c. butterscotch or peanut butter chips
1 c. cut walnuts
½ to ¾ can condensed milk
shredded coconut

Layer 1: Melt margarine in square pan (8 or 9-inch).
Layer 2: Cover margarine with graham cracker crumbs.
Layer 3: Sprinkle semi-sweet chocolate chips over crumbs.
Layer 4: Sprinkle butterscotch or peanut butter chips.
Layer 5: Spread walnuts over chips.
Layer 6: Drizzle condensed milk with a spoon over nuts.
Layer 7: Lightly sprinkle shredded coconut over condensed milk.
Bake at 350° for 25 minutes or until lightly browned. Store in refrigerator.

Butterscotch Bars

½ c. butter or margarine
2 c. brown sugar
2 c. flour
1 tsp. salt
2 tsp. baking powder
2 eggs
1 tsp. vanilla
1 c. peanuts, chopped (optional)

Melt butter, then stir in brown sugar; set aside to cool. Mix together flour, salt, and baking powder. Stir eggs into cooled brown sugar mixture, then blend in dry ingredients, vanilla, and peanuts. Spread in a greased 9 x 13-inch cake pan. Bake at 350° for 30 minutes.

Island Cookies

1⅔ c. flour
¾ c. baking powder
½ tsp. baking soda
½ tsp. salt
¾ c. butter, softened
¾ c. brown sugar
⅓ c. sugar
½ tsp. vanilla
1 large egg
1¾ c. milk chocolate chips
1 c. coconut
1 c. chopped walnuts

Preheat oven to 375°. Combine flour, baking powder, baking soda, and salt in small bowl. Beat butter, brown sugar, sugar, and vanilla in large bowl until creamy. Beat in egg. Gradually beat in flour mixture. Stir in chips, coconut, and nuts. Drop by slightly rounded tablespoonsful onto ungreased baking sheets. Bake for 8 to 10 minutes or until edges are lightly browned. Cool on baking sheets for 2 minutes. Place on wire racks to cool completely. YIELD: 3 dozen.

Mrs. Fields' Cookies

1 c. butter
1 c. sugar
1 c. brown sugar
3 eggs
1 tsp. vanilla
2 ½ c. oat flour (we grind oats in our blender)
2 c. flour
½ tsp. salt
1 tsp. baking soda
1 tsp. baking powder
12 oz. chocolate chips
4 oz. Hershey bars, finely grated
½ c. chopped nuts

Cream together butter, sugar, and brown sugar. Add eggs and vanilla. Combine oat flour, flour, salt, baking soda, and baking powder. Mix together all ingredients. Add chocolate chips and Hershey bars, finely grated. Add chopped nuts. Roll into golf-sized balls. Bake on ungreased cookie sheets at 375° for 6 minutes. *Very yummy!*

Chocolate Caramel Oat Bars

These are so good! Laura makes them for us for a special treat.

2¼ c. flour (divided)
2 c. oats
1 ½ c. brown sugar
1 tsp. baking soda
½ tsp. salt
1 ½ c. cold butter or margarine
2 c. (12 oz.) chocolate chips
1 c. chopped pecans
1 jar (12 oz.) caramel ice cream topping

In a bowl, combine 2 cups flour, oats, brown sugar, baking soda and salt. Cut in butter until crumbly. Set half aside for topping. Press the remaining crumb mixture into a greased 9 x 13-inch pan. Bake at 350° for 15 minutes. Sprinkle with chocolate chips and pecans. Whisk the caramel topping and remaining flour until smooth; drizzle over over top. Sprinkle with reserved crumb mixture. Bake for 18-20 minutes or until golden brown. Cool before cutting.

Whole Wheat Peanut Butter Cookies

½ c. oil
2 c. peanut butter
2 c. sugar
2 eggs
1 c. wheat germ
1 ½ c. oats
4 tsp. vanilla
12 Tbsp. water
1 ½ c. whole-wheat flour
2 c. dry milk powder
2 tsp. baking powder
3 tsp. baking soda

Cream together oil, peanut butter, sugar, and eggs. Add wheat germ, oats, vanilla, and water to creamed mixture. Combine the flour, milk powder, baking powder, and baking soda and add. Roll into 1-inch balls. Place on greased cookie sheet and flatten with fork dipped in flour. Bake at 375° for 8 to 10 minutes.

Congo Bars

This was one of my mom's recipes. I used to love to help her make these and "snitch" the batter at the same time!

⅔ c. shortening
1 lb. (2 c.) brown sugar
3 eggs
2 ⅔ c. flour
2 tsp. baking powder
1 tsp. salt
1 c. chopped nuts
1 tsp. vanilla
1 c. chocolate chips
¼ c. milk

Melt shortening in large saucepan. Let cool. Stir in sugar. Beat in eggs, one at a time. Stir in milk. Add flour, salt, and baking powder. Add nuts, vanilla, and chocolate chips. Spread batter into a greased 20 x 15-inch pan. Bake at 325° for 25 minutes.

Date, Nut, and Krispie Fingers

This is a favorite with my son Rick. The girls often make them for him for his birthday.

1 stick butter or margarine
1 beaten egg
1 c. granulated sugar
1 large c. chopped dates
2 c. Rice Krispies
1 tsp. vanilla
½ c. chopped nuts

In a large saucepan, combine butter, egg, sugar, and dates, and cook together for 10 minutes on low heat. Burns easily, so stir constantly. Add Rice Krispies, vanilla, and nuts. When cool enough to handle, form into small finger rolls and roll in coconut. Store in airtight container in refrigerator.

Maple Truffles

I always request these every year at Christmas. Emmy makes the best melt in your mouth maple truffles!

1 package (8 oz.) cream cheese, softened
½ cup butter, softened
6 cups confectioners' sugar
1 tsp. maple flavoring
2 pounds dark chocolate candy coating, coarsely chopped
1 c. chopped peanuts

In a large bowl, beat the cream cheese, butter, confectioners' sugar and flavoring until smooth. Cover and refrigerate for 1 hour.
Shape into 1-inch balls. In a microwave, melt candy coating, stirring often. Dip balls in coating; sprinkle with peanuts. Place on waxed paper-lined baking sheets. Refrigerate. YIELD: about 8 dozen.

Oreo Truffles

For the kids' birthday parties, we've even stuck lollipop sticks into completed balls and place in a container. I always request some of these for Christmas! An easy, but wonderful treat!

1 box cream cheese, softened
1 standard sized package Oreos
Milk or White Chocolate for dipping (we usually make some of each)*

*For the chocolate you can use either chocolate melts or almond bark.

Crush Oreos completely. We crush them in a blender. Mix thoroughly with cream cheese. Shape into balls and let chill. Dip in melted chocolate and let harden in refrigerator. Drizzle with white chocolate (optional).

Buckeyes

Foreground: Oreo Truffles. Background: Buckeyes

2 lb. peanut butter
1 lb. butter or margarine
3 lb. confectioners sugar
24 oz. semi-sweet chocolate chips, or dipping chocolate

Mix first three ingredients thoroughly to form stiff dough. Form into balls and dip in melted chocolate (which has been melted in a double boiler), leaving a little of the peanut butter ball showing at the top (see picture). Place on waxed paper and store in refrigerator. Makes about 250 balls.

Traditional Sugar Cookies

Twenty-two years ago, I purchased a set of Nativity scene cookie cutters. Every Christmas since then, I have baked these cookies with my kids, using those cutters. We always bring a batch to each of our neighbors' houses with a Christmas gospel tract and a bow on top.

¾ c. shortening (part butter or margarine), softened
1 c. sugar
2 eggs
1 tsp. salt
1 tsp. vanilla or ½ tsp. lemon extract
2 ½ c. all-purpose flour
1 tsp. baking powder

Mix thoroughly shortening, sugar, eggs, and flavoring. Blend in flour, baking powder, and salt. Cover; chill at least 1 hour. Heat oven to 400°. Roll dough ⅛-inch thick on lightly floured cloth-covered board. Cut into desired shapes. Place on ungreased baking sheet. Bake 6 to 8 minutes, or until very light brown. YIELD: about 4 dozen 3-inch cookies.

Spritz

This is another of our favorite Christmas cookie recipes. The kids enjoy using the cookie press to make their favorite designs.

1 c. butter or margarine, softened
½ c. sugar
2¼ c. flour
½ tsp. salt
1 egg
1 tsp. almond extract or vanilla

Heat oven to 400°. Cream butter and sugar. Blend in remaining ingredients. Fill cookie press with ¼ of the dough at a time; form desired shapes on ungreased baking sheet. Bake 6 to 9 minutes or until set but not brown. YIELD: about 5 dozen cookies.

Brownie Pudding

I came across this recipe as a newlywed and it quickly became one of Rick's favorites.

½ c. flour
1 tsp. baking powder
½ tsp. salt
⅓ c. granulated sugar
1 Tbsp. cocoa
¼ c. milk
1 Tbsp. shortening
½ tsp. vanilla
¼ c. chopped nuts
½ c. brown sugar
12 Tbsp. cocoa
¾ c. boiling water

Mix flour, baking powder, salt, sugar, and 1 tablespoon cocoa; sift. Add milk, shortening, and vanilla; mix only until smooth. Add nuts. Turn into greased casserole. Mix together sugar and remaining cocoa; sprinkle over batter. Then pour boiling water over top. This makes chocolate sauce in the bottom of the pan after pudding is baked. Bake at 350° for 30 to 40 minutes. YIELD: 6 to 8 servings.

Cheerios Treats

An easy, healthy treat. Kids love them.

3 Tbsp. butter or margarine
1 (10 oz.) pkg. mini marshmallows
½ c. peanut butter (smooth or crunchy)
5 c. Cheerios

Grease 9 x 13-inch pan. Melt margarine in a 3-quart saucepan on low heat. Add marshmallows and peanut butter; stir until marshmallows are melted and mixture is smooth. Remove from heat. Immediately add Cheerios; mix lightly until well coated. Press mixture into prepared pan. Cool. Cut into squares. YIELD: 24 bars.

Variations: Mix 1 cup M&M's or 1 cup raisins and ½ cup dry roasted peanuts with cereal. Add to warm marshmallow-peanut butter mixture.

Chocolate Trifle

Our daughter Carrie makes this for special gatherings. It has become a favorite.

1 ½ c. sugar
1 c. canola oil
1 c. milk
1 c. warm water
2 tbsp instant coffee granules
(more or less to suit tastes)
2 eggs
1 ½ tsp. vanilla extract
2 c. all-purpose flour
¾ c. baking cocoa
2 tsp. baking soda
1 tsp. baking powder
1 tsp. salt

In a large bowl, beat wet ingredients until well mixed. Add dry ingredients and beat until thoroughly combined. Pour into a 9 x 13-inch greased pan. Bake at 325° for approximately 35 minutes. Allow to cool. Meanwhile, prepare filling:

1 (16 oz.) container Whipped Topping, thawed
1 (8 oz.) pkg. cream cheese (let stand at room temperature for 20 minutes)
¾ c. powdered sugar

Beat cream cheese until smooth. Add powdered sugar and beat until combined. Add whipped topping and beat just until smooth.

Chocolate Ice Cream Topping
Caramel Ice Cream Topping

To assemble:

Cut cake into small squares. In trifle bowl, layer cake, then ⅓ to ½ jar of each ice cream topping and then half of the filling. Repeat layers. Top with drizzled ice cream toppings. YIELD: 12-16 servings.

Chocolate Pudding Dessert

When our seventh child was born, a friend from church brought a meal to us, including this delicious dessert. We got the recipe from her and it's become a favorite.

Bottom Layer:
1 ½ c. graham cracker crumbs
¼ c. sugar
½ melted margarine
Press into the bottom of a 9 x 13-inch pan. Chill 15 minutes.

Middle Layer:
8 oz. softened cream cheese
¼ c. sugar
2 Tbsp. milk
Whip until smooth. Fold in 1½ cups Cool Whip.

Top Layer:
2 small pkg. instant chocolate pudding
3 ½ c. milk
1 ½ c. Cool Whip
Prepare pudding using 3½ cups milk. Spread pudding over middle layer. Spread Cool Whip on top. Chill several hours. Refrigerate leftovers.

Brownies

This is my old standby favorite brownie recipe.

½ c. cocoa*
⅔ c. shortening
2 c. sugar
3 eggs
1 tsp. vanilla
1¼ c. all-purpose flour
1 tsp. baking powder
1 tsp. salt
1 c. chopped nuts (optional)

*May substitute 2 squares, 1 ounce each, unsweetened baking chocolate for the cocoa.

Melt shortening with cocoa; add sugar and cool slightly. Add eggs and vanilla; mix well. Stir in remaining ingredients. Pour into greased 9 x 13-inch baking pan. Bake at 350° until the edges start to pull away from sides of pan (approximately 20 minutes). Do not overbake! Cool; cut into bars.

Old Virginia Brownies

We have a wonderful neighbor who taught our kids piano lessons for free. Even the kids who didn't like playing the piano loved going up there because after each lesson, she had a special treat waiting for that student. My daughter Kate liked these so much as a child that she asked for the recipe and has made it many times since.

4 eggs
2 sticks margarine or butter
2 c. sugar
1 tsp. salt
1 tsp. vanilla
10 Tbsp. cocoa
1 ½ c. flour

Beat eggs; melt margarine. Add margarine to eggs in mixing bowl. Add all other ingredients except flour. Beat thoroughly. Add flour and mix thoroughly with wooden spoon. Spread in greased 9 x 13-inch baking pan. Bake at 350° for 30 minutes.

German Chocolate Brownies

German chocolate is one of my favorite things. My daughter Kate tasted these at a Creative Memories class she was teaching and got the recipe from one of her customers, the class coordinator.

1 box German chocolate cake mix
½ c. butter, melted
1 egg
1 can sweetened condensed milk
2 c. coconut
1 c. chocolate chips

Mix the cake mix, butter, and egg together in bowl. Spread in 9 x 13-inch greased baking pan. Cover with coconut, chocolate chips, and sweetened condensed milk. Bake for 30 minutes at 350°.

Buster Bar Dessert

1 lb. chocolate sandwich cookies
1 stick margarine, melted
½ gal. ice cream (let sit on counter to soften approximately 20 minutes)
2 c. powdered sugar
1 ½ c. evaporated milk
⅔ c. chocolate chips
½ c. butter
1 tsp. vanilla
1 ½ c. Spanish peanuts

Crush cookies; add margarine and press in the bottom of a 9 x 13-inch and 8 x 8-inch pan. Freeze 1 hour. Spread ice cream (flavor of your choice) over cookie crusts; return to freezer. In a saucepan, boil sugar, milk, chips, and butter for 8 minutes, stirring constantly. Add vanilla. Cool completely. Spread Spanish peanuts over ice cream; pour chocolate sauce over peanuts. Return to freezer until serving time.

Chocolate Meltaways

I first had a taste of these squares when I was in fourth or fifth grade and visiting my best friend. Her mother made these treats for us and I enjoyed them so much I asked her for the recipe. This family was my first exposure of the gospel.

½ c. butter
1 (1 oz.) sq. unsweetened chocolate
¼ c. sugar
1 tsp. vanilla
1 egg, beaten
2 c. graham cracker crumbs
1 c. coconut
½ c. chopped nuts

Melt butter and chocolate in saucepan. Blend sugar, vanilla, egg, graham cracker crumbs, coconut, and nuts into butter chocolate mixture. Mix thoroughly and press into 11½ x 7½ x 1½-inch or 9-inch square pan. Refrigerate while making filling.

Filling:
¼ c. butter
1 Tbsp. milk or cream
2 c. sifted confectioners' sugar
1 tsp. vanilla
1 ½ sq. unsweetened chocolate, melted

Cream butter, milk, sugar, and vanilla. Mix and spread over crumb mixture. Chill. Pour melted chocolate over chilled mixture and spread evenly. Store in refrigerator. Cut into squares before firm. YIELD: 3 to 4 dozen squares.

Open-Face Cherry Torte

2 c. flour
½ c. brown sugar
1 c. chopped nuts
1 c. butter
1 (8 oz.) pkg. cream cheese
1 c. confectioners' sugar
1 Tbsp. vanilla
1 small carton whipped topping
1 can cherry pie filling*

*Blueberry or strawberry pie filling may be substituted for cherry.

Mix flour, sugar, nuts, and butter until crumbly. Press mixture into 9 x 13-inch pan. Bake 15 minutes at 400°. Take a fork and crumble into pieces; press back into pan. Mix cream cheese, sugar, and vanilla. Add whipped topping and mix. Pour onto cooled crust. Top with pie filling. Chill 12 hours. YIELD: 16 servings.

Turtle Tart

My daughter Kate loves to bake and here is one of her many treats that have become a favorite.

Cookie Crust:

1 package oatmeal chocolate chip cookie dough mix (I use Betty Crocker)
½ cup butter, softened
1 tablespoon water
1 egg
1 cup chopped pecans

Mix ingredients together and press into a 9 or 10-inch tart pan with removable bottom. Bake at 350° for 19-21 minutes or until set. Cool for 10 minutes.

Caramel Filling:

40 caramels, unwrapped (I use Kraft)
⅓ cup whipping cream
¾ cup chopped pecans

Combine ingredients in microwavable bowl and microwave for 2-4 minutes, stirring twice. Spread over cooled crust. Refrigerate for 15 minutes.

Chocolate Topping:

1 bag (11.5 or 12 ounces) milk chocolate chips
⅓ cup whipping cream
¼ cup pecans

Microwave on high for 1-2 minutes, stirring every 30 seconds. Spread over top of caramel filling. Refrigerate for 2 hours. Let set 10 minutes before cutting.

Banana Pudding

This recipe came from a wonderful pastor's wife.

vanilla wafers
sliced bananas
1 large pkg. instant vanilla pudding, prepared
1 (16 oz.) carton sour cream
1 large container Cool Whip

Line 9 x 13-inch pan with vanilla wafers and sliced bananas on bottom and sides. Mix together pudding, sour cream, and Cool Whip. Spoon into dish on top of wafers. Arrange more sliced bananas on top. Refrigerate until serving time; refrigerate any leftovers. YIELD: 12 servings.

Caramel Squares

I found this recipe in a church cookbook that my aunt gave me one Christmas back when I was in high school.

Crust:

¾ c. butter
1 tsp. vanilla
¼ tsp. salt
2 c. flour
¾ c. confectioners' sugar, sifted
1 ½ Tbsp. milk

Cream butter, gradually adding sugar. Add vanilla, milk, and salt. Blend in flour; mix well. Spread in 9 x 13-inch pan. Bake 20 minutes at 350°.

Filling:

28 caramels
¼ c. butter
1 c. chopped pecans
¼ c. evaporated milk
1 c. sifted confectioners' sugar

Combine caramels and milk in top of double boiler. Heat until caramels melt, stirring occasionally. Remove from heat and add butter and sugar. Mix well after adding nuts; spread over crust.

Icing:

1 c. semi-sweet chocolate chips
¼ c. evaporated milk
2 Tbsp. butter
½ c. sifted confectioners' sugar
1 tsp. vanilla

Melt chips and milk; stir in remaining ingredients and mix well. Spread over caramel. Cool. Cut into squares.

No-Bake Blueberry Cheesecake

2 (8 oz.) pkg. cream cheese
1 c. sugar
1 pt. (2 c.) sour cream
1 can blueberry pie filling
1 pre-made graham cracker crust

Cream softened cream cheese and sugar. Whip in sour cream. Spoon into graham cracker crust. Chill for 2 hours; spread pie filling on top. Refrigerate until serving time. Other flavors of fruit pie filling may be substituted for blueberry. YIELD: 8 servings.

Turtle Cheesecake

My daughter-in-law Christina makes this recipes. She is a pro on cheesecakes.

pre-made graham-cracker pie crust
2 pkg. (8 oz. each) cream cheese, softened
½ cup sugar
2 tsp. vanilla
2 large eggs
¼ cup hot fudge topping
1 c. coarsely chopped pecans
1 Tbsp. butter
1 c. caramel topping

In large bowl, beat cream cheese, sugar, vanilla, and eggs with electric mixer on low speed until smooth. Reserve half of the mixture in separate bowl. Add hot fudge topping to cream cheese mixture in one of the bowls; beat on low speed until smooth. Alternating between bowls, spoon chocolate and vanilla mixtures into pie crust. Swirl mixtures slightly with tip of knife. Bake at 350° for 40 to 50 minutes or until center is set. Cool at room temperature 1 hour. Refrigerate at least 2 hours until chilled.

In small saucepan, heat chopped pecans and butter, stirring regularly, over medium heat until pecans are toasted lightly. Serve with caramel topping and toasted pecans. Store covered in refrigerator.

Aunt Betty's Quick Fruit Cobbler

This recipe came from Rick's Aunt Betty who lived on a Missouri farm. You can use with any type of fruit.

½ c. margarine
1 c. flour
1 ½ tsp. baking powder
1 c. sugar
¼ tsp. salt
¾ c. milk
3 c. fruit and juice
1 c. sugar
cinnamon and nutmeg

Melt margarine in bottom of 9 x 13-inch pan. In mixing bowl, combine flour, baking powder, 1 cup sugar, and salt. Add milk to dry ingredients, then pour over top of melted margarine. Do not stir. Add fruit and juice. Do not stir. Add 1 cup sugar on top. Do not stir. Add cinnamon and nutmeg on top. Bake at 350° for 40 to 45 minutes.

Whoopie Pies

These were some of our favorite cookies when my sisters and I were kids. Mom would bake the cookies and we would fill them.

2 c. flour
¼ tsp. salt
1 tsp. baking soda
⅓ c. cocoa
1 c. sugar
¾ c. milk
1 tsp. vanilla
1 egg
⅓ c. melted margarine

Sift flour, salt, soda, and cocoa together 3 times in a mixing bowl. Add sugar, milk, vanilla, egg, and margarine. Mix with electric mixer. Drop from a teaspoon onto an ungreased cookie sheet. Bake in 350° oven for 10 minutes.

Whipped Filling:

½ stick margarine
1 c. confectioners' sugar
½ jar Marshmallow Creme
1 tsp. vanilla

Mix in mixer. Spread between 2 cookies, making a sandwich. Repeat with remaining cookies and filling.(Filling recipe may also be used for filling chocolate cupcakes.)

Muddy Buddies

Rick's mom made this when she was here one time. The kids absolutely loved it and asked Grannie for the recipe, and have enjoyed making it since then.

¼ c. (½ stick) margarine
1 c. chocolate chips
½ c. peanut butter
9 c. flavor Chex cereal
1 ½ c. powdered sugar
1 tsp. vanilla

Pour cereal into large bowl; set aside. In a 1-quart microwave-safe bowl, combine chocolate chips, peanut butter, and margarine. Microwave on HIGH 1 to 1½ minutes or until smooth, stirring after 1 minute. Stir in vanilla. Pour chocolate mixture over cereal, stirring until all pieces are evenly coated. Pour cereal mixture into a large resealable bag. Add powdered sugar. Seal securely and shake until all pieces are well coated. Spread on waxed paper to cool. YIELD: 9 cups.

Hot Fudge Ice Cream Cake

This is often what I request Kate to make for Mother's Day. It tastes even better than Shoney's ice cream cake.

1 boxed devils food cake mix (18.25 oz.)
3 eggs
1 ⅓ c. water
⅓ c. vegetable oil
1 half-gallon box vanilla ice cream (must be in a box)
1 (16 oz.) jar chocolate fudge sauce
1 can whipped cream
12 maraschino cherries

Mix batter for the cake as instructed on box. Measure only 4 cups of batter into a well-greased 9 x 13-inch baking pan. Use remaining batter for cupcakes or another recipe if desired. Bake cake according to package directions; cool completely.

When cake has cooled, carefully remove it from pan and place it right-side up onto a sheet of waxed paper. With a long, serrated knife, slice horizontally through the middle of the cake and carefully remove the top. Pick up the waxed paper with the bottom of the cake still on it, and place it back into the baking pan.

Take ice cream from the freezer and, working quickly, tear the box open so you can slice the ice cream like bread. Make six ¾-inch thick slices and arrange them on the cake bottom in the pan. Cover entire surface of cake with ice cream, trimming ice cream slices as necessary to make it all fit. Carefully place the top half of the cake onto the ice cream layer so ice cream is sandwiched between cake layers. Cover the whole pan with plastic wrap or foil and freeze for a couple hours. (It will keep well for a couple weeks if needed as long as it is covered well and is airtight.)

To serve, slice the cake into 12 even slices. Let sit for 5 minutes to defrost slightly. Heat up the hot fudge sauce in microwave or in jar immersed in a saucepan of water over medium/low heat.

Pour the hot fudge over the cake slices and to each add a mountain of whipped cream and top with a cherry. YIELD: 12 servings.

Baked Custard

3 c. scalded milk
6 egg yolks or 3 eggs
½ c. sugar
¼ tsp. salt
few gratings of nutmeg

Beat eggs slightly. Add sugar and salt. Slowly pour on scalded milk; strain into buttered mold and set in a pan of hot water. Sprinkle with nutmeg. Bake at 350° until firm. Test with knife. When it comes out clean, custard is done. Don't let surrounding water boil or custard will whey.

Ice Cream Dessert

This is a delicious treat for summer (or anytime)! It's a favorite with company.

1 lb. Oreos
⅓ c. melted margarine
½ gal. vanilla ice cream
1 (1 oz.) sq. unsweetened chocolate
⅓ c. evaporated milk
¼ c. margarine
⅔ c. sugar
pinch of salt

Crush Oreos; mix with ⅓ cup melted margarine and press into a bottom of a 9 x 13-inch pan. Let ice cream stand at room temperature while preparing topping.

Topping:

Combine chocolate, milk, ¼ cup margarine, sugar, and salt in saucepan; boil 3 minutes. Cool completely. Spread ice cream over cookie crust. Drizzle topping over ice cream and freeze until serving time.

Chocolate chip, mint chocolate chip, cookies 'n' cream or other flavors of ice cream may be substituted for vanilla.

Cookies and Cream Ice Cream

For a special treat on hot summer days, we sometimes crank homemade ice cream. This is one of our favorite recipes.

1 small pkg. Oreo cookies
2 cans sweetened condensed milk
1 can evaporated milk
2 pt. half and half
1 tsp. vanilla
milk (to fill)

Grind up cookies, then mix it all together in ice cream freezer and crank until hard.

Ice Cream Cake

This delicious cake is similar to the ones you buy at Dairy Queen.

1 (1 lb.) pkg. Oreo cookies
½ stick melted butter or margarine
½ gal. vanilla or chocolate chip ice cream
1 large box dry instant vanilla pudding mix
Cool Whip

Crush the Oreo cookies and mix with melted butter or margarine. Spread in a 9 x 13-inch pan. Let ice cream soften then mix with dry pudding mix. Spread on top of Oreo cookie crust. Spread Cool Whip on top. Sprinkle with crushed Oreo cookies, if desired. Place in freezer until frozen.

Basic No-Churn Ice Cream

Christina's recipe. You can have fun experimenting with different additives with this very easy recipe. It's simple enough for even little children to help out!

1 pint heavy whipping cream
1 (14 oz.) can sweetened condensed milk

Combine ingredients in large mixing bowl. Using hand-held mixer or stand mixer, beat until stiff peaks form. Freeze overnight.

Variations: Add flavorings before beating: vanilla extract, Nutella, coffee, chocolate milk, etc. Make a concentrated version of your favorite drink, chill it, then add to the mixture before blending.

Add "toppings" after beating: chopped up candy bars, cookies, berries, nuts, toffee chips, etc. Fold gently into mixture after beating. For this amount, two Kit Kat bars and 6 sandwich cookies, coarsely chopped, made enough together to accommodate the ice cream generously.

Snow Cream

Every good snowstorm we have (which isn't too frequent here in Virginia!), we reserve a nice clean patch of snow with the promise of this treat in mind. We made up this recipe when our oldest boys were little, and everyone looks forward to when their dad makes this for us.

1 ½ to 2 c. sugar
2 Tbsp. vanilla
2 c. milk
2 eggs
3 qt. clean snow

Combine sugar, vanilla, milk, and eggs in saucepan. Boil until sugar is dissolved (about 5 minutes). Cool completely; set pan outside in snow to chill. When cold, combine syrup and snow, mix thoroughly. Serve immediately.

Homemade Strawberry Ice Cream

Kelley made this for us and it is so delicious! It doesn't use any cream, just whole milk. EASY! Extra good with fresh milk.

3 c. sliced strawberries or 3 heaping c. whole berries
1 ⅔ cups sugar
2 ½ c. whole milk (we used raw milk, but not necessary)
½ tsp. vanilla

Clean strawberries and slice. Blend strawberries, sugar, and milk in blender or food processor using the blade attachment. Pour strawberry mixture into ice-cream maker and process according to freezer's directions. Serve at once when processed or store in freezer.

Strawberry Pizza Pie

Every May, we go to the strawberry fields and pick lots of strawberries. We freeze some of the berries for later use but we always bake a couple of these pies that day.

½ c. powdered sugar
1 c. real butter
2 c. plain flour
8 oz. cream cheese
1 c. powdered sugar
9 oz. Cool Whip
2 pt. strawberries
1 c. sugar
4 Tbsp. cornstarch
4 Tbsp. water
1 tsp. vanilla
1 tsp. red food coloring

Crust:

Combine first 3 ingredients; mix well and press onto round pizza pan. Bake at 350° for 20 minutes. Cool.

Filling #1:

Whip cream cheese and 1 cup powdered sugar. Fold into Cool Whip. spread over chilled crust and chill while preparing next filling.

Filling #2:

Crush 1 pint strawberries and add sugar, cornstarch, vanilla, and water. Bring to a boil and add food coloring. Cook until thick and clear (about 1 minute). Slice another pint of berries and add to cooled filling. Spread this over the cheese filling and cover with dollops of Cool Whip. Garnish with whole berries. Chill. Slice into thin wedges.

Granola p. 137

Fruit Yogurt Pops p. 139

Hot Chocolate Mix p. 136

Beverages & Miscellaneous

Beverages & Miscellaneous

Hot Chocolate Mix

1 (25.6 oz) pkg. instant nonfat dry milk (10⅔ c.)
1 (6 oz.) jar powdered nondairy creamer
1 c. sugar
1 (16 oz.) can instant chocolate drink mix

Combine all ingredients in large bowl. Mix well; transfer to an airtight container. YIELD: 17 cups mix.
Add 3 tablespoons mix to 1 cup hot water for 1 serving.

Orange Julius

A great breakfast drink! My kids absolutely loved this. We made up the recipe years ago when an Orange Julius store opened up in our mall.

1 egg
⅓ c. concentrated orange juice
1 c. milk
4 to 6 ice cubes, crushed
1 to 2 tsp. sugar or honey (optional)

Combine all ingredients in blender. Blend until smooth. YIELD: 1 pint.

Variation: Substitute 1 banana plus ½ teaspoon vanilla or ½ cup sliced strawberries for orange concentrate.

Orange Juice Slush

This is a yummy, nutritious frothy drink. It's almost like an "icee," only this is good for you! My son Tim came up with this recipe. You might want to try it with different juices, too.

Place ice cubes in blender. Cover with orange juice. Add 1 teaspoon vanilla; blend until smooth.

Mocha Punch

This is a favorite for Thanksgiving/Christmas night at our home. After a big midday dinner we eat desserts and drink mocha punch for an evening treat.

1½ qts. water
½ c. instant chocolate drink mix
½ c. sugar
¼ c. instant coffee granules
½ gal vanilla ice cream
½ gal. chocolate ice cream
1 c. whipped cream

In a large saucepan, bring the water to a boil. Remove from heat. Add drink mix, sugar, and coffee; stir until dissolved. Cover and refrigerate for 4 hours or overnight. About 30 minutes before serving, pour into a punch bowl. Add ice cream by scoopfuls; stir until partially melted. Garnish with dollops of whipped cream. YIELD: 20–25 servings—approximately 5 quarts.

Holiday Punch

1 package (6 oz.) cherry Jello
¾ c. sugar
2 c. boiling water
1 can (46 oz.) pineapple juice
6 c. cold water
2 liters ginger ale

In a 4 qt. freezer-proof container, dissolve Jello and sugar in boiling water. Stir in pineapple juice and cold water. Cover and freeze overnight. Remove from freezer 2 hours before serving. Place in a punch bowl; stir in ginger ale just before serving. YIELD: 32–36 servings (5¾ qt.)

Granola

Dry Ingredients:

wheat germ
sunflower seeds
sesame seeds
pumpkin seeds, roasted
fresh grated or dried coconut
dry milk solids
chopped nuts
spices (cinnamon, nutmeg, etc.)

Preheat oven to 300°. Combine in large bowl 7 cups dry ingredients including at least 2 to 3 cups rolled oats plus other grains and nuts as desired.

continued on page 138

GRANOLA *continued*

One Cup Liquids:

honey
syrup
molasses
brown sugar
(use 2 Tbsp. water with ½ c. brown sugar)
oil
melted margarine
peanut butter
milk

Combine separately and pour over dry ingredients 1 cup liquid. Bake in large greased baking pans 30 to 60 minutes, stirring often. Do not over-brown. Crunchiness depends on proportions and baking time. For a chunkier granola, allow to cool undisturbed, then break into pieces. Add when cool, as desired, raisins, chopped dates, apricots, or other fruits.

EASY CHEWY GRANOLA BARS

These are Laura's specialty. Good and good for you! High in fiber

2 c. whole oats
2 c. Rice Krispy cereal
¼ c. flax seed
½ c. honey
½ c. brown sugar
½ c. peanut butter
1 c. mix-ins (mini chocolate chips, dried fruit, etc...)

Note from Laura: I cut the sugar and chocolate chips in half, and you couldn't tell the difference! Also added a little extra flax to increase the fiber.

In a large bowl, mix together the oats, cereal, and flax. Set aside. In a medium saucepan, combine the honey and sugar. Stir over medium heat until sugar completely dissolves. Once dissolved, remove from heat and add the peanut butter. Add to oats mixture and add mix-ins of your choice. Pour immediately into waxed paper lined 9 x 13-inch pan. Press firmly into pan to an even thickness. Cool completely, then cut into bars. Store in an airtight container.

Yogurt Pops

These make a wonderful, nutritious summertime snack.

1 pt. plain yogurt
1 tsp. vanilla
6 Tbsp. (½ small carton) frozen orange juice concentrate

Blend until smooth. Freeze in popsicle molds. When partially frozen, insert wooden sticks.
Optional: Substitute frozen grape or pineapple concentrate. We also make juice pops for summer; just freeze plain juice in pop holders. Insert wooden sticks when partially frozen. Freeze until firm.

Fruit Yogurt Pops

We make these all summer long. They're nutritious and the kids and adults love them. We can't keep enough made up! We use all different types of fruit, fresh or frozen.

⅔ c. yogurt
2 generous Tbsp. honey
1 c. strawberries or other fruit

Put yogurt in blender. Turn on low and add 1 strawberry at a time until smooth. Add honey and blend. Freeze in popsicle containers.

Raspberry Pops

1 (3 oz.) pkg. raspberry flavored gelatin
1 c. boiling water
1 (8 oz.) carton raspberry yogurt

Dissolve gelatin in boiling water. Chill until partially set. Add yogurt and beat with electric mixer. Pour into six 3½-ounce paper cups. Freeze. When partially frozen, insert wooden sticks. Freeze until firm. YIELD: 6 pops.

Blueberry Pops

1 (8 oz.) carton blueberry yogurt
2 c. blueberries

Combine in blender; blend until smooth. Pour into six 3½-ounce paper drinking cups. partially freeze. Insert wooden sticks. Freeze until firm. YIELD: 6 pops.

Frozen Fruit Cups

We were introduced to this recipe at my son Tim's wedding. Kari and her mom had made these and frozen ahead to serve the guests. Delicious and convenient as you can make ahead and thaw as needed.

1 can frozen orange/pineapple juice
1 c. water
½ c. sugar
2 tsp. lemon juice
3 bananas, sliced
1 (16 oz.) frozen strawberries (2 cups)
2 (15 oz.) cans mandarin oranges
1 big can crushed pineapple

Prepare juice according to package directions. Add water, sugar, and remaining ingredients. Pour into plastic disposable punch cups. Freeze. Thaw 15 to 20 minutes before serving. Makes approximately twelve 9-oz. cups.

Snack Mix

Great nutritious snack. Kids love to make it!

Mix 1 cup each chocolate chips, peanuts, sunflower seeds, and raisins. Store in airtight container.

Trail Mix

Another nutritious snack, easy and enjoyable for the kids to make.

1 box Chex rice cereal
1 box Chex corn cereal
1 box Chex wheat cereal
raisins
chocolate chips
peanuts

Mix all ingredients. Store in airtight containers.

Quick and Easy "Cracker Jacks"

¼ c. margarine or butter
½ c. honey
6 c. popped popcorn
1 c. peanuts

In saucepan over low heat, stir honey and margarine just until blended. In large bowl, mix popcorn and peanuts. Add sauce; stir. Spread mixture into 2 large pans. Bake at 350° for 7 to 10 minutes. When cool, stir. Store in airtight container.

Play Dough

This is my favorite play dough recipe. I have plastic knives, molds, rolling pins, cookie cutters, etc. It entertains the little ones for long periods of time. I often let the youngest ones use play dough while I "do school" with the older kids. It's not crumbly like store-bought play dough.

1 c. flour
2 tsp. cream of tartar
1 c. water
½ c. salt
few drops of food coloring (optional)
3 Tbsp. oil

Mix and cook in saucepan on medium heat until mixture coagulates into a ball. Cool. Store in airtight container.

Crayon Circles

broken crayons
shortening or margarine

Grease muffin tins with shortening and line with disposable baking cups. Break up the crayons to no more than ½-inch in length and place in baking cups. Turn the oven to 250°. Put the muffin tins in the oven and check them after about a minute. When they are melted together into a circle shape, take them out of the oven. Let them cool, then take them out of the tin.

Dough Ornaments

4 c. presifted all-purpose flour
1 c. iodized salt
1½ c. warm water

Mix flour and iodized salt. Add water and mix until dough no longer sticks to the sides of bowl. Then knead the dough on lightly floured surface about 10 minutes until smooth. Work with half the dough at a time, keeping the rest in a plastic bag (may be refrigerated for a week or frozen). Return to room temperature and knead before use.

Roll dough ¼ to 3/8-inch thick. Use floured cookie cutters. Immediately use nail to make hole for hanging. Use spatula to lift onto cookie sheet. Bake at 150° for several hours. Then air dry or leave in oven overnight with oven off. Sand edges smooth. Paint as desired and then spray with glossy varnish spray or craft spray. Store in dry place or tissue wrap in tin box for safety. If broken, mend with white all-purpose glue. Will keep for many years.

Play Clay Christmas Tree Ornaments

2 c. (1 lb.) baking soda
1 c. cornstarch
1¼ c. cold water

Stir together baking soda and cornstarch in saucepan. Add water and cook over medium heat, stirring constantly. When mixture is the consistency of moist mashed potatoes (approximately 10 to 15 minutes), turn out on a plate and cover with a damp cloth. As soon as clay cools enough to handle, gently pat it until it's smooth. Clay is now ready to use. If desired, you may store unused portions in a tightly sealed plastic bag in the refrigerator, but remember to bring them to room temperature before using.

Roll out clay to ¼-inch thickness on waxed paper. Cut with cookie cutters into circles, stars, Christmas or animal shapes. Use a toothpick to press a hole near the top for hanging ornament with a string.

When the ornaments have been cut out, place them on a plate, cookie sheet, or other flat surface. Thin designs should harden overnight. Thick designs may need more time. To shorten drying time, ornaments on a cookie sheet can be placed in a preheated oven at lowest setting for 10 to 15 minutes. Or, microwave at medium power on a paper towel, 30 seconds per side. Continue to turn ornaments until dried. Let ornaments cool before handling.

Coloring:

Solid color clay can be made by adding a few drops of food coloring to the water before it is mixed with the baking soda and cornstarch. For bright glossy colors, paint hardened pieces with water colors, poster paints, or acrylic paints. Glitter can be applied to wet paint, or later, with craft glue. Felt tip pen can also be used for drawing on details.

Decorating:

Patterns can be pressed into soft clay with paper clips or kitchen utensils. Cut out smaller shapes or roll bits of clay into small balls and moisten, then press onto larger cutouts. If any designs come loose after drying, reapply with craft glue.

Finishing:

Ornaments can be protected with a shiny glaze. You can dip them into clear varnish, coat them with liquid plastic, or paint them with one or two coats of clear nail polish. Wrap seasonal objects carefully and store in a safe place as they will break if dropped.

Index of Recipes

APPETIZERS, JAMS & PICKLES

SOUPS, SALADS & SAUCES

MEATS & MAIN DISHES

VEGETABLES

BREAD, ROLLS & PASTRIES

CAKES, COOKIES & DESSERTS

BEVERAGES & MISCELLANEOUS

Ingredient Substitutions

ITEM	AMOUNT	SUBSTITUTION
Allspice	1 teaspoon	½ teaspoon cinnamon plus 1/8 teaspoon ground cloves
Baking powder	1 teaspoon	¼ teaspoon baking soda plus 5/8 teaspoon cream of tartar
Bread crumbs, dry	¼ cup	1 slice bread
Bread crumbs, soft	½ cup	1 slice bread
Butter *Rule:* Don't use spreads or low-fat butter in baking	1 cup	⅞ to 1 cup hydrogenated fat (shortening) and ½ teaspoon salt ⅞ cup lard plus ½ teaspoon salt 1 cup margarine ⅞ cup oil plus ½ teaspoon salt To reduce fat and calories: applesauce or prune puree for half of the butter recipe
Buttermilk	1 cup	1 cup plain yogurt
Chocolate, unsweetened	1 ounce	3 tablespoons cocoa plus 1 tablespoon butter or fat
Chocolate chips, semi-sweet	1 ounce	1 ounce sweet cooking chocolate 1 ounce unsweetened chocolate plus 1 tablespoon sugar
Chocolate chips, semi-sweet, melted	6 ounce package	2 squares unsweetened chocolate, 2 tablespoons shortening, and ½ cup sugar
Chocolate, semi-sweet	1 ⅔ ounces	1 ounce unsweetened chocolate and 4 teaspoons sugar
Cocoa powder, natural, unsweetened	3 tablespoons	1 ounce (square) chocolate (decrease fat called for in recipe by ½ tablespoon) 3 tablespoons Dutch-processed cocoa plus 1/8 teaspoon cream of tartar, lemon juice, or white vinegar 3 tablespoons carob powder

ITEM	AMOUNT	SUBSTITUTION
Cornstarch (for thickening)	1 tablespoon	2 tablespoos all-purpose flour 2 tablespoons granulated tapioca 1 tablespoon potato or rice starch 1 tablespoon arrowroot 4 teaspoons instant tapioca
Cracker crumbs	¾ cup	1 cup dry bread crumbs
Cream, heavy	1 cup	¾ cup milk plus ⅓ cup melted butter (this will not whip)
Cream, light	1 cup	⅞ cup milk plus 3 tablespoons melted butter
Cream, sour	1 cup	⅞ cup buttermilk or plain yogurt plus 3 tablespoons melted butter
Cream, whipping	1 cup	⅔ cup well-chilled evaporated milk, whipped; or 1 cup nonfat dry milk powder whipped with 1 cup ice water
Flour, all-purpose	1 cup	1-1/8 cups cake flour; or 5/8 cup potato flour; or 1-¼ cups rye flour or coarsely ground whole-grain flour; or 1 cup cornmeal
Flour, cake	1 cup	1 cup minus 2 tablespoons sifted all-purpose flour
Flour, self-rising	1 cup	1 cup all-purpose flour plus 1-¼ teaspoons baking powder plus ¼ teaspoon salt
Garlic	1 small clove	1/8 teaspoon garlic powder or instant minced garlic
Herbs, dried	½ to 1 teaspoon	1 tablespoon fresh herbs, minced and packed
Honey	1 cup	1-¼ cups sugar plus ½ cup liquid
Lemon	1	½ teaspoon vinegar
Lemon, juice and rind	1	3 tablespoons bottled lemon juice and 1 teaspoon dried grated rind
Lemon rind, grated	1 teaspoon	½ teaspoon lemon extract
Macaroni (4 cups cooked)	2 cups uncooked	2 cups spaghetti, uncooked 4 cups noodles, uncooked

INGREDIENT SUBSTITUTIONS

ITEM	AMOUNT	SUBSTITUTION
Marshmallows, minature	1 cup	8 to 10 large marshmallows
Mayonnaise (for use in salads and salad dressings)	1 cup	½ cup yogurt and ½ cup mayonnaise 1 cup either yogurt, salad dressing, or sour cream 1 cup cottage cheese pureed in blender
Milk, evaporated (whole or skim)	1 cup plus	1 cup liquid whole milk 1 cup regular cream, whipping, or heavy cream
Milk, skim	1 cup	⅓ cup instant nonfat dry milk plus ¾ cup water
Milk, sour	1 cup	1 cup minus 1 tablespoon milk plus 1 tablespoon vinegar or lemon juice. Stir and let stand 5 minutes
Milk, sweetened condensed	1 can (about 1⅓ cups)	Heat the following ingredients until sugar and butter are dissolved: ⅓ cup plus 2 tablespoons evaporated milk, 1 cup sugar, 3 tablespoons butter or margarine
Milk, whole	1 cup	½ cup evaporated milk plus ½ cup water; or 1 cup skim milk plus 2 teaspoons melted butter
Mustard, prepared	1 tablespoon	1 teaspoon dry or powdered mustard
Onion, chopped	1 small	1 tablespoon instant minced onion; or 1 teaspoon onion powder; or ¼ cup frozen chopped onion
Sour cream, cultured	1 cup	¾ cup sour milk and ⅓ cup butter or margarine ¾ cup buttermilk and ⅓ cup butter or margarine Blend until smooth: ⅓ cup buttermilk, 1 Tbsp. lemon juice, and 1 cup cottage cheese 1 cup plain yogurt ¾ cup milk, ¾ tsp. lemon juice, and ⅓ cup butter or margarine

ITEM	AMOUNT	SUBSTITUTION
Sugar, granulated	1 cup	1 cup firmly packed brown sugar; or 1¾ cups confectioners' sugar (do not substitute in baking); or ½ cup honey; or 1 cup superfine sugar; or 1½ cups corn syrup; or ⅔ cup maple syrup (for last two, reduce liquid in recipe by 25 percent)
Sugar, brown (light or dark)	1 cup firmly packed	1 cup granulated sugar 1 cup granulated sugar plus ¼ cup unsulphured molasses ½ cup liquid brown sugar 1 cup raw sugar
Tomatoes, canned	1 cup	½ cup tomato sauce plus ½ cup water; or 1⅓ cups chopped fresh tomatoes, simmered
Tomato juice	1 cup	½ cup tomato sauce plus ½ cup water plus dash each salt and sugar; or ⅓ cup tomato paste plus ¾ cup water plus salt and sugar to taste
Tomato ketchup	½ cup	½ cup tomato sauce plus 2 tablespoons sugar, 1 tablespoon vinegar, and 1/8 teaspoon ground cloves
Tomato puree	1 can (10¾ oz.)	1 cup tomato sauce plus ¼ cup water
Yeast	1 cake (3/5 oz.)	1 package active dry yeast
Yogurt, plain	1 cup	1 cup buttermilk; or 1 cup cottage cheese blended until smooth; or 1 cup sour cream

Weights & Measures

dash = 2 to 3 drops
3 teaspoons = 1 tablespoon
4 tablespoons = ¼ cup = 2 fluid ounces
8 tablespoons = ½ cup = 4 fluid ounces
12 tablespoons = ¾ cup = 6 fluid ounces
16 tablespoons = 1 cup = 8 fluid ounces

2 cups = 16 fluid ounces = 1 pint
4 cups = 32 fluid ounces = 1 quart
4 quarts = 1 gallon
8 quarts = 1 peck
4 pecks = 1 bushel
16 ounces = 1 pound